Microsoft Azure Security

Protect your solutions from malicious users
using Microsoft Azure Services

Roberto Freato

professional expertise distilled

BIRMINGHAM - MUMBAI

Microsoft Azure Security

First published: April 2015

Production reference: 1310315

Published by Packt Publishing Ltd.
Livery Place
35 Livery Street
Birmingham B3 2PB, UK.

ISBN 978-1-78439-997-9

www.packtpub.com

Credits

Author

Roberto Freato

Reviewers

Jignesh Gangajaliya

Christos Matskas

Marco Parenzan

Naveen Kumar Vijayakumar

Commissioning Editor

Amarabha Banerjee

Acquisition Editor

Reshma Raman

Content Development Editor

Samantha Gonsalves

Technical Editor

Gaurav Suri

Copy Editor

Sonia Michelle Cheema

Project Coordinator

Kinjal Bari

Proofreaders

Simran Bhogal

Ameesha Green

Bernadette Watkins

Indexer

Mariammal Chettiyar

Graphics

Valentina D'silva

Disha Haria

Abhinash Sahu

Production Coordinator

Manu Joseph

Cover Work

Manu Joseph

About the Author

Roberto Freato has been an independent IT consultant ever since he started working. He worked for small software factories while he was studying; after an MSc degree in computer science engineering and a thesis on consumer Cloud computing, he specialized particularly in Cloud computing and Azure. Currently, he works as a freelance consultant for companies in Italy, helping clients to design and kickoff their distributed software solutions. He conducts training sessions for the developer community in his free time, giving lectures at conferences. He has also been a Microsoft MVP since 2010.

I would like to thank Simona, and my mom and dad.

About the Reviewers

Jignesh Gangajaliya is a principal technical architect with over 11 years of core technology and global business leadership experience in defining solutions and technology architectures.

His expertise lies in leading design, development, and deployment of large-scale software systems, and solutions across various industry verticals. His core strengths include wide and deep hands-on technological expertise, strategic thinking, comprehensive analytical skills, creativity in solving complex problems, and the ability to quickly understand complex business problems and come up with pragmatic solutions.

He is passionate about creating a strategic vision, building and transforming organizations to accelerate growth, and value creation by leveraging new technologies, trends, and emerging opportunities.

He specializes in enterprise architecture, solution architecture, Microsoft product servers and technologies, Cloud computing, SaaS, Microsoft Azure, and Amazon Web Services.

Christos Matskas is a software developer who has worked professionally for the last 11 years. He is an entrepreneur, founder, and CEO of Softwarelounge, a software consultancy firm, and cofounder of TowzieTyke, an applications development powerhouse. His portfolio includes collaborations with some great companies, such as MarkIT, Lockheed Martin, and Barclays. Over the years, he has worked on numerous exciting projects, ranging from mobile apps to data crunching backend solutions. His blog, `https://cmatskas.com`, is full of useful tutorials, tips and tricks, and reviews on software development tools. Christos also contributes to open source initiatives, and is a regular speaker at conferences and user groups, where he talks about .NET, Cloud, mobile applications, and software development in general.

I would like to thank my beautiful and charismatic wife for supporting me in this role and my kids for inspiring me to be a better person.

Marco Parenzan has been a .NET programmer since 2001, and is now a Cloud programmer too. He loves software architectures and writing code. He likes programming functions and games in his spare time. He was given the Microsoft MVP award for Azure in 2014. He provides training to companies and universities, in Friuli Venezia Giulia (Italy). He is a speaker for 1nn0va, a Microsoft community in Pordenone (refer to `http://www.innovazionefvg.net/`).

I want to dedicate this work to my wife, Paola, and to my children, who have always given me the time to do this. I'd also like to thank Roberto for giving me the opportunity to review his book.

Naveen Kumar Vijayakumar is a Amazon Web Services certified solutions architect. His keen interests lie in designing and architecting Cloud-based applications from the ground up and making existing applications (systems) Cloud-able. He also has experience in working in Microsoft Windows Azure Cloud Platform and Office 365. His hobbies include browsing the latest events in Tech Space, participating in forums, such as Stack Overflow, tweeting (his Twitter handle is `@navcode`), and blogging (visit `www.navcode.info`). He also loves to travel. Naveen holds a master's degree in information technology from IIIT, Bangalore, and is currently working for Digital Intelligence Systems (DISYS) as a Cloud architect.

www.PacktPub.com

Support files, eBooks, discount offers, and more

For support files and downloads related to your book, please visit www.PacktPub.com.

Did you know that Packt offers eBook versions of every book published, with PDF and ePub files available? You can upgrade to the eBook version at www.PacktPub.com and as a print book customer, you are entitled to a discount on the eBook copy. Get in touch with us at service@packtpub.com for more details.

At www.PacktPub.com, you can also read a collection of free technical articles, sign up for a range of free newsletters and receive exclusive discounts and offers on Packt books and eBooks.

https://www2.packtpub.com/books/subscription/packtlib

Do you need instant solutions to your IT questions? PacktLib is Packt's online digital book library. Here, you can search, access, and read Packt's entire library of books.

Why subscribe?
- Fully searchable across every book published by Packt
- Copy and paste, print, and bookmark content
- On demand and accessible via a web browser

Free access for Packt account holders

If you have an account with Packt at www.PacktPub.com, you can use this to access PacktLib today and view 9 entirely free books. Simply use your login credentials for immediate access.

Instant updates on new Packt books

Get notified! Find out when new books are published by following @PacktEnterprise on Twitter or the *Packt Enterprise* Facebook page.

Table of Contents

Preface

The purpose of this book is, on one hand, to introduce how security should be interpreted, and, on the other hand, to identify the security hot spots while using the Microsoft Azure platform as users and developers.

Microsoft Azure is Microsoft's platform for Cloud computing. It provides developers with elastic building blocks to build scalable applications. These building blocks are services for web hosting, storage, computation, connectivity, and more, which are usable as standalone services or can be mixed together to build advanced scenarios.

In this book, we will try to learn how security should not be delegated to fancy tools or to all-in-one salvation software, but it is primarily related to creating *awareness* among people involved in business processes. Companies should (and must) implement internal procedures to assess themselves from a security perspective, documenting the risks they are subjected to, and the measures used to mitigate (if necessary) these risks.

Microsoft Azure is an evolving platform. Technical topics have a high decay rate, so Azure Services are also enriched on a daily basis with new features and service models, making the goal of writing a complete book almost impossible. However, this book focuses on core concepts that remain quite stable over time.

What this book covers

Chapter 1, The Fundamentals of Security Standards, shows you how security principles are often related to common sense (and to a good understanding of a few core concepts) and how they can be achieved during the whole process. This chapter could also be a great introduction to certain security definitions for those who are not familiar with them.

Chapter 2, Identity and Access Management for Users, shows you the Identity and Access Management mechanisms used to control the resources of the Azure platform, by discussing IAM (short for Identity and Access Management) and advanced authentication. This chapter is essential for anyone who wants to start using Azure at a good level of security.

Chapter 3, Platform as a Service, shows you the most important Azure PaaS building blocks and highlights the security aspects of websites, Cloud Services, storage, SQL Database, caches, and Service Bus. This chapter helps while implementing solutions using the PaaS blocks of Azure.

Chapter 4, Infrastructure as a Service, shows you the most important Azure IaaS building blocks and highlights the security aspects of Virtual Machines and Virtual Networks, and also introduces the Azure Backup service. This chapter helps while implementing solutions using the IaaS blocks of Azure.

Chapter 5, Identity and Access Management for Developers, shows you how to use Azure Active Directory in custom applications, which are the integration scenarios, and gives an introduction to advanced features, such as Azure Key Vault. This chapter is particularly useful when implementing Identity in applications and dealing with secrets and keys.

What you need for this book

This book requires a basic exposure to the main concepts of Microsoft Azure, as well as C# programming language, and Visual Studio IDE. The software needed to practice on are Visual Studio 2013, with the latest Azure SDK, and Azure PowerShell.

Who this book is for

If you want to understand how security principles apply in distributed environments, how Azure provides security, and most importantly, how to use Azure to its best capability to reduce the risks of security breaches, then this book is for you. This book is ideal for developers who don't have a lot of confidence while using Azure security services, but desire to learn more.

Conventions

In this book, you will find a number of styles of text that distinguish between different kinds of information. Here are some examples of these styles, and an explanation of their meaning.

Code words in text, database table names, folder names, filenames, file extensions, pathnames, dummy URLs, user input, and Twitter handles are shown as follows: "If you have multiple subscriptions, list them with the `Get-AzureSubscription` cmdlet."

A block of code is set as follows:

```
{
  "sku" : {
    "family" : "A",
    "name" : "standard"
  },
  "tenantId" : "[…]",
  "accessPolicies" : [
    {
      "tenantId" : "[…]",
      "objectId" : "[…]",
      "permissions" : {
        "secrets" : ["all"],
        "keys" : ["get", "create", "delete", "list", "update",
        "import", "backup", "restore"]
      }
    }
  ],
  "enabledForDeployment" : false,
  "vaultUri" : "https://[name].vault.azure.net/"
}
```

Any command-line input or output is written as follows:

```
Set-AzureKeyVaultAccessPolicy -VaultName [vaultName] -
  ServicePrincipalName [clientID] -PermissionsToSecrets all
```

New terms and **important words** are shown in bold. Words that you see on the screen, in menus or dialog boxes for example, appear in the text like this: "On the bottom menu, click on the **MANAGE MULTI-FACTOR AUTH** button."

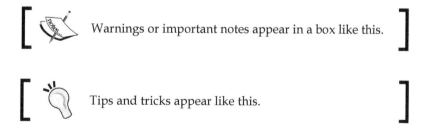

Warnings or important notes appear in a box like this.

Tips and tricks appear like this.

Reader feedback

Feedback from our readers is always welcome. Let us know what you think about this book—what you liked or may have disliked. Reader feedback is important for us to develop titles that you really get the most out of.

To send us general feedback, simply send an e-mail to feedback@packtpub.com, and mention the book title via the subject of your message.

If there is a topic that you have expertise in and you are interested in either writing or contributing to a book, see our author guide on www.packtpub.com/authors.

Customer support

Now that you are the proud owner of a Packt book, we have a number of things to help you to get the most from your purchase.

Errata

Although we have taken every care to ensure the accuracy of our content, mistakes do happen. If you find a mistake in one of our books—maybe a mistake in the text or the code—we would be grateful if you would report this to us. By doing so, you can save other readers from frustration and help us improve subsequent versions of this book. If you find any errata, please report them by visiting http://www.packtpub.com/submit-errata, selecting your book, clicking on the **errata submission form** link, and entering the details of your errata. Once your errata are verified, your submission will be accepted and the errata will be uploaded on our website, or added to any list of existing errata, under the Errata section of that title. Any existing errata can be viewed by selecting your title from http://www.packtpub.com/support.

Piracy

Piracy of copyright material on the Internet is an ongoing problem across all media. At Packt, we take the protection of our copyright and licenses very seriously. If you come across any illegal copies of our works, in any form, on the Internet, please provide us with the location address or website name immediately so that we can pursue a remedy.

Please contact us at copyright@packtpub.com with a link to the suspected pirated material.

We appreciate your help in protecting our authors, and our ability to bring you valuable content.

Questions

You can contact us at questions@packtpub.com if you are having a problem with any aspect of the book, and we will do our best to address it.

1
The Fundamentals of Security Standards

Before we get down to talking about Azure specifically, we need to gather some basic information about what *security* means in the context of information technology, where it is often called information security. In this chapter, we are going to talk about the following topics:

- Information security fundamentals
- Physical measures versus logical measures
- Security standards and Azure

In this chapter, we will show how these security principles are often related to common sense (and to a good understanding of a few core concepts) and how they have to be achieved during the whole process. Here, the *process* is a comprehensive end-to-end series of tasks involved in information management, and not only the usage of Azure technology.

Information security fundamentals

Let's start with a brief recap of high school concepts, such as the difference between data and information. In many cases, both should be treated as important assets, though there is an important difference.

Data is the raw piece of a fact, which describes something; information is the output of a process of elaboration of raw data.

> Think about a sensitive digital document containing strategic company plans. If someone sees the raw bits of this document, no one could probably gain any kind of advantage from it. Instead, if these bits (the data) are properly translated by some software into a human-readable document, information is generated.

I mentioned that both of these are important, since raw data can produce a lot of information. However, it is generally accepted that information has much more value as it represents the output of a high value transformation process.

CIA triangle

It is probably well known that the most widely-accepted principles of IT security are confidentiality, integrity, and availability. Despite many security experts defining even more indicators/principles related to IT security, most security controls are focused on these principles, since the vulnerabilities are often expressed as a breach of one (or many) of these three. These three principles are also known as the **CIA triangle**:

- **Confidentiality**: This is about disclosure.

  A breach of confidentiality means that somewhere, some critical and confidential information has been disclosed unexpectedly.

- **Integrity**: This is about state of information.

  A breach of integrity means that information has been corrupted or, alternatively, the meaning of the information has been altered unexpectedly.

- **Availability**: This is about interruption.

  A breach of availability means that information access is denied unexpectedly.

Ensuring confidentiality, integrity, and availability means that information flows are always monitored and the necessary controls are enforced.

We say that a **breach** means an exposure, which is caused by an event that occurred when exploiting a vulnerability located in some point of the involved process.

> Those events are often called **incidents**, since they expose a system to loss or damage. Later, we you learn how to identify the threats of a system, which is one of the main purposes of **Information Security Management (ISM)**.

As you can see from the the three principles discussed, for each security principle we need to ensure that information flows are always monitored and the necessary controls are enforced. The first is a basic milestone of information security, since all the information flows have to be known and documented by an officer in order to plan which controls should be enforced. The second part, instead, is related to a specific principle; security measures vary from one principle to another, as follows:

- The examples of the measures for confidentiality are:
    - Applying classification signs on a company's documents could help people understand which grade of secrecy is applied.
    - Applying a *deny-all* policy and allowing only a minimal set of permissions to users will reduce the risk of a loss of confidentiality.

- The examples of the measures for integrity are:
    - A data validation policy for users involved in data entry or data manipulation helps to reduce the probability of errors and, consequently, a loss of integrity.
    - Continuous backups could mitigate the damage of data corruption, by restoring the most recent and consistent version of data.

- The examples of the measures for availability are:
    - Having at least two power sources for critical IT infrastructure increases the availability of a system in case damage is suffered by one of them. This is an example of **redundancy**.
    - Again, backups can be also be viewed as measures to increase availability since, in the case of a hardware failure, a good backup procedure could reduce the downtime dramatically.

Sometimes we encounter other principles related to security, such as non-repudiation, authenticity, utility, possession, and more. I prefer to reduce all the principles to the CIA triangle, since I think the other ones are specializations of this base model.

Security management

In this book, we will try to teach you that security should not be delegated to fancy tools or to all-in-one salvation software, but it is primarily related to the awareness of people involved in business processes. Companies should (and must) implement internal procedures to assess themselves by a security perspective, documenting the risks they are subjected to and the measures to mitigate (if necessary) these risks.

This is, in summary, the purpose of a Security Management System which, when talking about IT, becomes an **Information Security Management System (ISMS)**.

In the previous sections, we talked about risks, vulnerabilities, threats, and incidents; now let us try to give an example.

A company hires sales representatives, giving them a PC with essential tools of trade, **Customer Relationship Management (CRM)** access, and a database of clients with their details (that is, the past revenues). The person in charge of security decides to force users in mobility to use a **Virtual Private Network (VPN)** to connect to the company network and to choose a strong password for the desktop access. However, if the PC's hard drive is not fully encrypted, the company is *vulnerable* to loss of confidentiality, in the case of theft or loss; the *threat* is that someone could attach the hard drive to another PC and read all the plain data. The *risk* associated with this event is the likelihood of a sales representative losing the PC or a thief stealing it, regardless of using the information contained in it. The *measures* in this case could be at least two: avoid saving sensitive data on the PC, making it a stateless device (or thin client), or performing a full disk encryption. In both cases, someone taking physical access and ownership of the device cannot take advantage of the information contained in it.

In this example, we used the appropriate terminology to describe a typical real-world scenario. Please note that security controls (or measures) could themselves lead to new risks. Imagine a company policy that forces each PC to be encrypted with a key. In the case of the user losing this key, the PC would become useless even for people who have the right to access it. Again, if the disk key is a number, writing it down on the back cover of the PC completely avoids the benefit introduced by the encryption policy (a thief could steal both the PC and the key, gaining access to the device's sensitive information). These are two cases when measures to ensure confidentiality introduce new risks related to availability and confidentiality.

This is one of the reasons why a planned, documented, and formal ISMS is really needed by most companies who are dealing in information.

> The process of understanding, assessing, and documenting current threats and risks is often known as **due diligence**, while the actual implementation of these measures to protect the company from threats is known as **due care**.

Medium or big companies approach ISM by appointing a dedicated staff member as the **Information Security Officer (ISO)**, who is usually in charge of a division (or a small portion of a company), and a **Chief Information Security Officer (CISO)**, who is usually in charge of implementing the security strategy for the entire company.

Why are dedicated staff needed to implement security?

Although the implementation of ISMS seems a like one-time task, it is, in fact, a continuous process of iterative improvement, based on the monitoring of the actual procedures, that have been placed as a result of the previous implementation. As in software development, it is hard to say "it's finished" for a particular piece of software; rather, when a software has been released, new functionalities or fixing must be made accordingly to new business requirements. In ISM, it is the same.

Risk analysis

A threat should not always be contrasted; regarding the previous example, if the possible loss in the PC costs of the sales representative (in terms of the information lost) is less than the measure to fight against this threat (by implementing proper measures), the company could accept the risk. Today, it is often very cheap to protect a PC (through encryption, for instance), but there are other cases where it would be convenient to avoid an expensive implementation. This conclusion can be made only after a documented process of analysis.

As per the book *Foundations of Information Security, Van Haren* by Jule Hintzbergen, Kees Hintzbergen, Andre Smulders, and Hans Baars, a risk could be accepted or mitigated by five kind of countermeasures: preventive, reductive, detective, repressive, and corrective measures.

Coming back to the previous example, we may face this situation:

- A PC with sensitive data is given to an employee
- A thief could steal it (or the employee could lose it)

A *preventive* measure would make this an impossible risk; for example, by avoiding giving PCs to the employees. A *reductive* measure would reduce the likelihood of the risk, by forcing the employees to be always be hard connected to their devices. A *detective* measure helps to promptly realize that an incident has occurred, by placing some localization device on the PC, which is somehow connected to a real-time tracking system. A *repressive* measure would limit the consequences of an incident, for example, by remote wiping the stolen (or lost) PC. Finally, a *corrective* measure would recover the consistent state before the incident, by providing a new PC for the employees. As previously said, a risk could also be accepted. In such cases, no countermeasures are taken, but the risk should be documented as well.

Physical measures and logical measures

Now, we will see which measures could be placed to manage the risks related to information security, dividing them into this classification:

- **Physical measures**: These measures involve some kind of physical infrastructure (smaller or bigger), which protects sensitive resources

- **Logical measures**: These measures are achieved by logical implementations (new or modified business processes and software implementations)

> Some people split logical measures into technical (related to IT stuff) and organizational (related to processes). However, for the purpose of this book, this classification is enough.

Introducing ISO/IEC 27000

The **International Organization for Standardization (ISO)** and the **International Electrotechnical Commission (IEC)** often work together to build international standards around specific technical fields. They released the ISO/IEC 27000 series to provide a family of standards for ISMS, starting from definitions (ISO/IEC 27000) up to governance (ISO/IEC 27014) and even more. Two standards of particular interests are the ISO/IEC 27001 and the ISO/IEC 27002. The first has been released to define the requirements to build an ISMS, while the second has been released to provide controls (or measures) to help companies implement an effective ISMS, as described in the 27001 document.

>
> International standards should be transposed to the actual requirements of a specific environment; they provide a framework supporting the process of building an effective ISMS, while they are not prescriptive at all. However, companies that adhere to the guidelines of these international standards are less exposed to unexpected exceptions, giving the entire company an added sense of trust and robustness.

Physical security and controls

Physical security is the part of information security that is probably well known by anyone. Since it protects an asset physically, we have all probably dealt with it in our lives in many circumstances, such as how do we protect a building, how do we protect a car, and how do we protect cash? First, we will try to physically protect these resources from outside access with simple or sophisticated security measures.

Security boundaries

With information security, we start from the assumption that we have something similar to a server farm to protect against damage or thieves. Therefore, what should we do to enforce security?

We cannot answer this question without knowing the following initial conditions:

- Where is the server farm building located?
- Are there some fences/gates to cross to get into the building area or not?
- How far is the building from the nearest police station (or private security office)?
- Is the building outside an area monitored for suspicious activities?

Answering these questions is, in fact, a part of the ISMS process itself. Providing a good description of the initial conditions helps to build measures to mitigate risks. Let's proceed to going into the building with other questions:

- Is the building entrance properly supervised?
- Is there a key (or an identification) to get into the building?
  - ° Could that key/ID be copied easily?
  - ° Could someone else use that key/ID?
- Is there a proper security control for loading/unloading areas?

Please note, we are not yet into the working space and we already have many security issues to manage. Let's proceed, going at the top floor where the server farm is:

- Is the server farm room protected against intrusion?
- Are there any proper intrusion detection systems (alarms or sensors)?
- In case of an unexpected breach, is there a process to block the company in order to reduce the risk of losing data (and to catch the thief)?

We are just talking about measures to prevent unauthorized access to sensitive assets for people who do not have the right to be there. However, we should also consider other risks:

- Could the legitimate administrator shut down the power source of the server farm?
  - ° Or they should be at least two power sources at the same time?
- Is the server farm room properly furnished with fire extinguishers?

- Are incoming post parcels properly scanned to detect prohibited materials, explosives, and dangerous goods?

Many security measures seem as though they're evidence of the paranoia of the CISO. However, not every possible measure should be implemented since, as we said before, a company could also accept the risk, or reduce it to another one.

As mentioned previously, each answer (and consequently each countermeasure) could lead to a new risk. The purpose of an ISMS is also to set up a continuous improvement process to find and manage new risks properly.

Exercise for you:

Is the new monitoring system installed in the whole company to protect the assets compliant with local laws and regulations? Have proper actions to legally film employees been done?

Mobile equipment

In the previous example, we talked about ways to protect a hypothetical server farm against unauthorized access or disasters such as fire. Those considerations are still valid for on-premise equipment that is stable fastened in company offices, such as cabling, desks, and big workstations. These are examples of what a thief could not easily steal (because of the weight and risk involved).

Imagine now how sensitive a CEO's desktop is in terms of confidentiality of information: documents, laptops, and smartphones might contain business secrets and losing them could lead the company into disaster too.

Protecting mobile resources with physical measures means applying new measures to provide security even outside it, in addition to the safety measures that are already implemented in the company.

Smartphones are like mini-PCs with saved credentials, sensitive web browser history, financial data, and e-mail accounts, and the risk of losing this data is mainly related to the mobility of the owner.

Let's consider an agent travelling with his or her mobile equipment. These are some of the questions that may arise pertaining to the physical security of this equipment:

- Is the smartphone always (when not in use) enclosed in a container (pocket, bag, or pack)?
    - ° Is it protected from falls and shocks by a proper shell or cover?

- Are sensitive paper-based documents enclosed in plastic sealed envelopes to protect them from water?

- Does the agent have a second power supply to operate his or her PC in case of low battery?

These three questions give examples of what physical security for mobile devices could be:

- The first is about confidentiality (protecting the smartphone against loss) and availability (protecting it from breakage)

- The second is about integrity (a wet document may be compromised)

- The third is about availability (an agent without his or her operational PC can waste time and money)

Logical security and controls

Logical security is something that is not a physical measure to enforce security, such as access control, cryptography, organizational security processes, conventions, and many more. In this section, you will completely understand how ISMS is a pervasive approach, defining almost everything that is somehow related to the security of information.

Human resources

Enforcing personnel security starts when the HR department evaluates a new candidate to hire in the company. First, the department should perform adequate *screening* of the candidate by verifying the information he or she is showing to the company in the resume. If the research gives an evidence of the candidate's insincerity, this is, of course, a negative component in the overall evaluation.

Also, the *reliability* of a candidate should be taken into consideration, mostly if he or she has to work with sensitive information, or is in contact with high-profile employees. Verify the truthfulness of the information declared by the candidate, which is again a good index of evaluation, especially if the entities who recommend him or her are certified or well known.

Another aspect strongly related to information security is the ability for an employee to disclose what he or she receives from the company as long as he or she works for it. Actually, the problem is still valid even after a person is outplaced, since the secrecy of the company information remains. By using **Non-Disclosure Agreements (NDA)** with employees, even if the company cannot solve the problem, it can reduce the risk of someone publicly disclosing the information.

During the working lifetime of employees, the company must train them to adhere to internal regulations, for example, the security policies about information technology. Government laws hardly recognize the validity of companies' internal policies and code of conduct; they can be used to create awareness and, in the case of failure of an employee, they can be used to raise the appropriate disciplinary process.

A **code of conduct** is a document (or a set of documents) used to state the responsibilities of an employee regarding the best practices to enforce minimal security measures, that are implemented by a company. A code of conduct may deny the use of social networks during work time, since social engineering can extract sensitive information from people's activities feed.

Access control

When someone talks about IT and software security, respectively, the first topic is always access control. **Access control** is a logical measure to guarantee that only authorized entities can access private resources.

New employees of a company are provided with certain security tokens, such as keys, badges, security cards, and so on to allow them access to specific physical and logical resources. At the end of the work relationship, they must be prevented from access to the company resources by the company revoking them.

Access control is also a physical measure, similar to badges or biometrics, while entering a building or a restricted area.

Almost every access control system uses *credentials* to identify and authorize users. Credentials are a couple of objects: the first identifies the user (or entity) and the other (that is very private) is like a key shared between the user and the system. In complex IT infrastructures, managing the credentials of a company is not an easy task to maintain. To reduce the risks connected to credential management, it is often recommended to use a centralized system of *identity management* (that is, Active Directory), which is useful to issue/delete credentials and to grant/revoke permission, especially when **Role-Based Access Control (RBAC)** is in use.

While using a centralized system for identity management reduces some risks, it also introduces new ones, as previously stated in this chapter. The system administrator now has the capability to grant extra powers to unauthorized users, and can access the company's protected data. Therefore, the new measures that rise to reduce these risks in the company are:

- Independent *auditing* can be done for every administrative task (this is a detective measure)

- A *multifactor authentication* (biometrics) could be enforced to compel the administrator to be physically at the office to operate

- An *approval process* (two administrators) could be set to perform a double check on administrative tasks

Access control is the very first measure to protect data, but the ability to recover lost credentials (in a short amount of time) is important too, to avoid unavailability or **Denial of Service (DoS)**.

Mobile devices

With the spread of mobile devices, new risks have arisen in security. First of all, losing the device can compromise company trade secrets, even if the device is found and used by someone who is not going to use the sensitive information. However, from an IT security perspective, the issue still remains.

Many modern mobile operating systems (that is, iOS, Android, and Windows phones) have a sort of built-in security system to protect themselves from misuse. Unlocking the screen by entering a passcode could be an effective entry-level protection. However, an experienced technician who wants to recover personal data can open the device and connect to its memory to manually recover the private data. Under these conditions, a full disk encryption is advised to prevent this circumstance.

 In recent years, many companies are adopting the **Bring Your Own Device (BYOD)** philosophy. It is a strategy that, on one hand, can let companies save money for the acquisition and maintenance of devices and, on the other hand, introduce a series of risks associated with the potential loss of governance around personal devices. In these cases, a trade-off between what an employee knows and what he or she can store on devices is required. Under these circumstances, digital services, such as intranet and e-mail are usually blocked by design.

This is similar to desktop computers and laptops. While in most cases, a thief would steal them to resell them somewhere, the possibility of a hard inspection is concrete and a full disk encryption is a good (and often, easy) solution to achieve.

 Many modern mobile operating systems also provide the capability to *remote wipe* the mobile device. This is a good solution to erase the contents of the device but it is available only if, after the loss, the device is reconnected to a network.

As usual, a new measure introduces new risks, such as what if the cryptography key is lost and who should be in charge (in a company) of the key management? We will discuss this in a later section.

 Inventory management process is required as a measure to correctly address the problem of tracking and monitoring the actual assets of mobile devices distributed to employees. Only through an accurate and planned process of inventory management can companies know at a given point of time which resources are in/out and who the current owner is.

Cryptography

Most of you probably know what encryption is. If we have a sender and a receiver, assuming the channel is unsafe (someone is listening), **encryption** transforms the message into another one with no semantic meanings until the receiver has received it, when it then comes back to the original form.

Symmetric encryption stands upon these concepts:

- The sender and receiver know a key
- Using a well-known algorithm, the sender encrypts the message with the key
- Using the same reverse algorithm, the receiver decrypts the message

This method, unfortunately, assumes that both parties possess the same key before the communication, and this exchange must be made in a secure manner. If this assumption is wrong, asymmetrical encryption can help. In *asymmetric encryption*, the sender has a public key and the receiver a private key. The public key is used to encrypt the data, while the private key is used to decrypt the data. Only the receiver can decrypt the data, so:

- The sender needs to send a message to the receiver; therefore, it asks for the receiver's public key

- With this key, the sender sends the encrypted message through the channel
- The receiver uses its private key to decrypt the message

If the public key is lost or intercepted, someone could just encrypt messages, not decrypt them. A *man-in-the-middle* behaves like the receiver, giving the sender its public key so it knows what it wants to send.

Public Key Infrastructure (PKI) is required when we want to correctly identify who the speaker at the other side of the cable is. With PKI, a sender can verify the identity of a receiver, while, for example, it gives back its public key to start an encrypted conversation. With PKI, the sender asks an authority the correctness of the information received by the receiver before it starts the communication process. HTTPS is an example of how PKI is used in Internet communication.

Communication

Communication is probably the key value of any company today. Sending an e-mail to a supplier or a colleague exposes the company to the risk of an information leak, if no security measures are taken.

 A specific internal regulation is needed while working with third parties operating on behalf of the company (that is, outsourcing), and a *fortiori* when these third parties need access to sensitive information.

The following questions can help you to understand which risks are concrete:

- Is the **Instant Messaging (IM)** system implementing a proper cryptography strategy to handle messages between parties?
    - Is the software used trusted?

- What is permitted to be sent by e-mail? Are there policies to filter incoming and outgoing messages, based on content, attachment, or sender/destination?

- Are people properly informed about what to disclose? Are they aware of which communication channel they can use to share the company's sensitive data?

Managing communication safely is harder than replying to these questions, but it is out of the scope of this book.

Software management

Giving IT equipment to employees exposes the company to a huge number of risks if they are permitted to install and use arbitrary software. This is why modern operating systems have sophisticated mechanisms to configure usage policies in order to permit/deny users to perform specific operations. However, configuring and maintaining the devices of a medium (or big) company one by one is not a simple task to perform. This is why it is recommended that you implement a centralized management system for devices and operating systems, performing administrative tasks in batches from a remote location.

If you do not have a clear understanding of how important software management is, please note the following:

- What if a user needs a new software? A proper process should be documented, where, for example, the user asks IT to install the software, and they, after validating the request, perform the remote installation of the requested tool.

- What if a user opens a virus or, generically, a malware application from the e-mail? Users should not have the proper rights to compromise the operating system. However, proper software restrictions in execution, Internet browsing, and content filtering could help to reduce the risks.

Exercise for you:

What about updates? Should users be independent while applying them? Why not? Is it a security issue or just a governance one?

Laws and regulations

A company should produce appropriate documentation about its processes to identify risks. As we said earlier, a good code of conduct should be distributed and adhered to by, by employees to build organizational ethics. Internal regulations must be presented to third parties, contractors, and external entities (who have business relationships with the company) to rule the connection and treatment of sensitive information.

These principles are real but first, a company should address local laws and regulations, such as:

- What are the code of conduct, the regulations, and the policies that are compliant with the law?

- Is every piece of software used compliant with local laws and regulations?
    - ° If not, what action could be implemented to replace them?

- Are the employees informed properly about laws and regulations, on top of the company's rules, to reduce the risk of them making mistakes?

Every country defines its own laws and regulations, for example:

- In some places, encryption is considered forbidden in some applications
- In some places, filming employees or visitors is considered illegal, even with a notice
- In some places, using location tracking on a company's devices given to users, is not permitted

IT security must include also the defects of local laws and regulations, for example, the patents or the rights contained within **Intellectual Property (IP)**. Different countries treat software patents differently; for an international company, choosing where to develop software could shape the future of the company itself.

The same applies to IP. There are countries where everything an employee produces (in terms of IP) during his or her work is the property of the company; other countries have different rules. So, as local regulations may differ, proper contracts and agreements should be made to create a common framework that can be used for an international company operating worldwide.

Security in software development

We covered security while using software, but what can we say about building it? The process of creating software hides a series of potential threats that must be addressed correctly before starting the development process. As usual, documented procedures and policies are the main tools a company can use to correctly map each vulnerability with every measure, to control (and reduce, where possible) the risks.

Local development tools

A developer often uses tools that require administrative access to the local machine (think about local web servers); also, during development, a new tool (or set of tools) needs to be installed quickly to perform an immediate action without asking for support. Finally, the operating system itself may be custom configured to test the software infrastructure created.

In some companies, speed is generally preferred over quality. In these environments, inexperienced developers must perform their work on top of every other administrative task (configuring networks, operating systems, and more). It may happen that a wrong configuration may lead the system into an inconsistent state, exposing the local environment (if not the entire network) to malicious software or external attackers.

The importance of a well-known, verified, and approved base set of development tools is important for a software development company; starting from this, the exceptions can be defined and the proper process to extend or upgrade a developer's permissions must be implemented.

Access to source code

If a company operates as a software house, the most important asset is code: how can we manage it safely? There is no a unique answer to this question, nor a procedure to avoid leaks. Of course, there are some suggestions:

- Is the code stored or checked in a code repository? A source code repository helps to granularly grant permission to a particular subset of the codebase on a user-by-user basis.

- Is the code repository publicly available on Internet? If not, an employee cannot use/dump the codebase from another PC or outside the company's premises. If it does, an employee can even work outside the company or leak the sensitive data.

A safe environment could be a **Virtual Machine (VM)** (accessible only from inside the company through a remote desktop solution) with the development tools and source code access. By denying Internet access and the copy/paste functionality from/to the VM, a company can reduce the risk of code leaks.

Credentials management

Except when we are working in the perfect company, developers usually gain access to sensitive data or, at least, much more than normal users. It is common to share the database credentials with the main developer, thinking that he or she is reliable. This is probably true but the problem is, by design, this means giving inadequate (or excessive) access to someone.

 A person with administrative access is an administrator and they can, in addition to operating sensitive data, make new administrators or change the existing ones.

In the rest of the book, we will discuss what it means to be an administrator of an Azure-based environment and we will look into different ways you can use to minimize the risk of security incidents.

Security standards in Azure

Microsoft manages the Azure infrastructure. At the most, users can manage the operating system inside a VM, but they do not need to administer, edit, or influence the under the hood infrastructure. They should not be able to do that at all.

Therefore, Azure is a **shared environment**. This means that a customer's VM can run on the same physical server of another customer and for any given Azure Service, two customers can even share the same VM (in some **Platform as a Service (PaaS)** and **Software as a Service (SaaS)** scenarios).

From the point of view of a customer, a shared environment could sound bad but also good, since there less is to manage and fewer errors might rise. As a consequence of this, Microsoft manages some rings of security, pursues other goals, and the availability of the shared environment.

Incidents and business continuity:

Incidents may occur, even for super-skilled people who are working in a Microsoft Azure **datacenter**. Incidents are caused by human faults (pressing the wrong button, inadvertently stumbling upon a power generator with coffee, and so on), by software bugs (a piece of code of a VM management tool crashes on January 1), and by a mix of both (a user forgot to renew an SSL certificate, which leads to the unexpected behavior of the application). When an incident occurs, the consequence could be a downtime in the customers' services. If the incident is not properly addressed, it could lead to a disaster.

Microsoft Azure, like many Cloud computing suites, guarantees a **Service Level Agreement (SLA)** on its building blocks. The key focus of the SLA is not *what happened* to the system, but how much time the system was unavailable in a given timeframe (usually a year). This indicator is measurable and it is also a contractual constraint, which is financially backed.

SLA is directly connected to business continuity: an e-commerce operator's interest is to reduce the risk of unexpected periods of unavailability that cause immediate loss of profits.

Implementing security, privacy, and compliance

Microsoft Azure implements the most recognized standards about security and privacy and implements effective practices about compliance. The **Microsoft Azure Trust Center** (http://azure.microsoft.com/en-us/support/trust-center/) highlights the attention given to the Cloud infrastructure in terms of what Microsoft does to enforce security, privacy, and compliance. Let's discuss these in detail.

Security

Part of Microsoft's attention to security is also about processes and management, by implementing a series of measures:

- **Security centers**: Microsoft implemented internal units for security, such as the Microsoft Digital Crimes Unit, Microsoft Cybercrime Center, and Microsoft Malware Protection Center

- **Security Development Lifecycle** (**SDL**): Microsoft implemented SDL to provide a software development process that is more secure from a security perspective

> More information about SDL can be found here: http://www.microsoft.com/security/sdl/default.aspx, including a training path to implement our own process.

- **Incident task force**: Microsoft documentation often states that infrastructures are designed to react, assuming there is a breach, fielding a *task force* of security experts who are available 24 x 7

The first point of interest is the management of the datacenter, where Microsoft takes care of everything including:

- **Physical security**: Microsoft assures that the datacenter buildings are designed to be monitored and controlled in the case of physical attacks (environmental or criminal).

- **Software updates**: For each managed service running on Azure (PaaS and SaaS services, at least), Microsoft applies the latest security updates (as long as there is malware protection), in order to avoid security breaches to its customers.

- **Hacking countermeasures**: Azure implements techniques to detect software intrusions and **Distributed Denial of Service** (**DDoS**) attacks, and performs periodic penetration tests to constantly ensure these requirements are met.

- **Isolation**: Since resources are shared, isolation between tenants (customers, but also different subscriptions) is implemented by design. Network activity between VMs is restricted (except the cases intentionally left for customers solutions).

In the rest of the book, we will discuss what we should do to implement security from a user perspective; while Azure manages the datacenter, users must manage the application's security.

Privacy

Microsoft Azure is a public Cloud product so, to ensure adoption, it must adhere to most of the security and privacy standards and/or regulations to be used worldwide. We can choose our own region to store applications and data and Microsoft assumes that for the services implementing geo-replication, data won't ever leave the geo-political area.

 What does the term geo-political area mean? Let's, for example, choose west Europe as the location for our deployment. In some cases, Microsoft, to ensure availability, creates replicas in another datacenter, preventing the supposed downtime in the case of a disaster in the primary one. However, a customer would not want the data replicated outside the political boundaries he or she has chosen. This is why there are often (at least) two datacenters in the same political region (that is, in Europe) where rules are accordant.

While privacy is also enforced at the personnel level (no one inside Microsoft can access resources, except for customers who request assistance), Microsoft offers strong contractual agreements to the enterprise customers and does not use data to sell advertisements anywhere.

Compliance

Previously in the chapter, you saw how security is mostly about processes instead of technology. We introduced the importance of standards, while implementing the proper controls and measures to be adequately safe. While avoiding unnecessary details, you must know that Microsoft Azure is certified for ISO/IEC 27001, while it is audited yearly.

Summary

In this chapter, we introduced IT security issues and also covered how a security officer should think while facing this aspect. We looked at the ISO standards and covered some security controls to help you understand what a Cloud vendor does and to better understand what we have to do.

In the next chapters, we only talk about Azure and we focus on the processes instead of the technology. In the next chapter, we talk about Identity and Access Management from the user's perspective by implementing security controls in the authentication process.

2
Identity and Access Management for Users

Microsoft Azure is a comprehensive set of services used to build complex infrastructures on Cloud Services.

In this chapter, we are going to explore the **Identity and Access Management (IAM)** mechanisms to control the resources of the Azure Platform, while discussing the following:

- IAM in the current portal
- IAM in the Preview portal
- Advanced authentication

Despite the definition of *old* and *new*, a portal can suggest which one is the future of a platform. In this chapter, we will cover both, so as to let users decide which one to use.

Microsoft Azure Management Portal is a web-based application where Azure subscribers usually go to manage their Cloud resources.

The first Management Portal was a Silverlight-based portal, now no longer used, and it has been replaced with a fully featured web-based application, which is available at `https://manage.windowsazure.com`. This *old* portal (at the time of writing this book, it is the current portal) is the main entry point for a majority of the services of the Azure Platform.

Recently, Microsoft developed a new portal (sometimes called *Ibiza*, the code-name, or just Preview portal) which features a completely renovated interface and is more focused on DevOps. This *new* portal is available at `https://portal.azure.com`, and Microsoft has stated that the coming features will be added to this portal only. Its new IAM features are discussed in this book in the following sections.

IAM in the current portal

The current portal, located at `https://manage.windowsazure.com`, is accessible with a valid credential, a Microsoft account, or a company account (hosted on Azure Active Directory). For users who do not have a valid subscription, the steps to get it are:

1. Obtain a valid Microsoft account (or create it at `https://signup.live.com`).

2. Go to `https://account.windowsazure.com/Subscriptions`.

3. Click on **add subscription**.

4. Choose the appropriate subscription (as shown in the following figure):

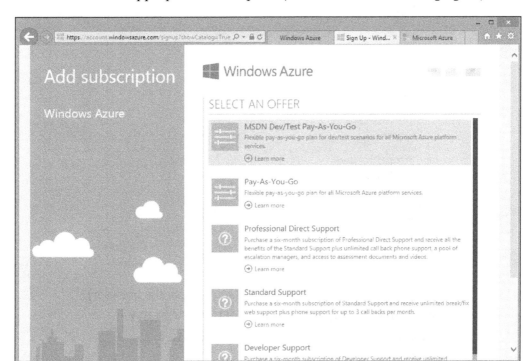

5. Verify the account (with a valid identification method; it depends on the subscription) and confirm it.

6. Go to the **Azure Portal** (refer to `https://manage.windowsazure.com`).

Once we are in the **Azure Portal**, the new subscription is added to the default directory of the owner's account (if any) or to an auto-generated one, if it was the first subscription or the user has not yet created a custom directory.

Creating a custom Azure Active Directory

It is a good practice to group multiple subscriptions (related to the same organization or logic group) into the same Azure **Active Directory** (**AD**). To do this, proceed as follows:

1. Go to the **ACTIVE DIRECTORY** tab of the **Azure Portal**.

2. Select **NEW | ACTIVE DIRECTORY | DIRECTORY | CUSTOM CREATE**.

3. A pop up will appear, fill it as follows:

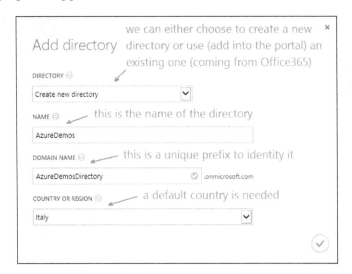

4. Once created, go to the **SETTINGS** tab (and refresh the browser).
5. Identify the subscription and click on **EDIT DIRECTORY**:

6. The browser will refresh. Now, in the **SUBSCRIPTIONS** menu, select the newly created **DIRECTORY**.

Properly organized subscriptions and directories are a good starting point while managing the access control to the Azure infrastructure. As we will see in the advanced section, the correct usage of AD enables several security scenarios.

It is very common that different people within the same organization would access and use the same Azure resources. In this case, a few scenarios arise: with the current portal, we can add several co-administrators; with the Preview portal, we can define fine grained **Access Control Lists** (**ACLs**) with the RBAC features it implements.

Configuring the Azure Directory user access

By default, we can add external users into the Azure AD, by inviting them through their e-mail addresses, which must be either a Microsoft account or an Azure AD account. To modify this behavior, we can go to the current portal in the **CONFIGURE** tab of the selected directory and locate the **user access** group, as follows:

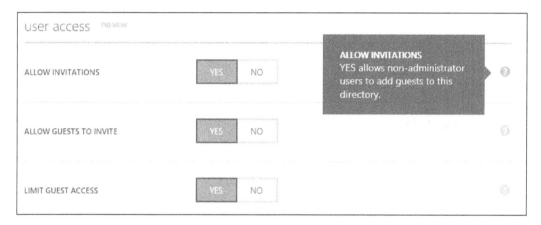

The three options shown in the preceding screenshot are for:

- Allowing non-administrator users to add guests to the directory
- Allowing guest users to add, and, in turn, also adding other guests to the directory
- Limiting the guest users from accessing the directory data

> **Create users and groups**: In the **USERS** and **GROUPS** tab, we can respectively, create new users or groups for the directory. A new user will be in the form, `username@directory.onmicrosoft.com` (or `@customdomain`), while a new group will be in the form of a security group with **MEMBERS** and **OWNERS**. A security group can be used later to grant access to resources in the RBAC engine of the Preview portal.

Adding a co-administrator to the subscription

A co-administrator (as the name suggests) is a user who has, like administrators, a huge control over the subscription. Co-administrators can do almost everything, such as:

- Having access to every Azure resource (within the subscription)
- Seeing/changing every access key of each Azure Service
- Creating/destroying resources
- Adding new co-administrators and removing them (even if they are created by someone else, including the main administrator)
- Removing themselves as co-administrators
- Adding/removing management certificates

They cannot, however, do the following:

- Remove the main administrator
- Change the directory of the subscription

This means that a co-administrator can do almost everything and, of course, they can create potentially unlimited new resources (and also generate costs) or destroy the entire infrastructure in a few minutes.

Apart from this, a co-administrator has a very useful role in many scenarios, and this role can be configured as follows:

1. Go to the **SETTINGS** tab of the **Azure Portal** and select **ADMINISTRATORS**.
2. Click on **ADD** in the menu at the bottom.
3. Enter a valid Microsoft account or a directory user and select the subscription to enable it.

Finally, we also need to know that adding a co-administrator (with a Microsoft account) will create an external user inside the Azure AD. This is also why in the previous section, in step 5, we show that a change in the directory removes co-administrators. A co-administrator must be a user in the **SUBSCRIPTIONS** directory. However, this does not expose the directory to security issues.

Securing the Microsoft account

While creating a new Microsoft account through e-mail, as a basic security measure, an alternative e-mail address is requested to reset the security information. This is a very basic measure to protect the account from malicious users trying to access it. In the past, it was easy to infer the correct information about the user's profile, through a secret question or birthday information, so today this stuff is not considered a good quality standard anymore.

In the 90s, Microsoft acquired a company called Hotmail, which in a few years, gained millions of users, giving them a free e-mail account with the @hotmail.com domain suffix. The number of users kept increasing and Microsoft offered this high bulk of users one of the biggest projects that it had ever made: a centralized authentication service providing a single sign-in for even third-party web applications. Originally, the service (known as *Microsoft Passport*, and then *Microsoft Live ID*) was connected to specific services and domains (such as passport.com, live.com, and hotmail. com) but now we can create a Microsoft account based on every valid e-mail address.

We can use a Microsoft account to manage Azure; however, it is strongly suggested that you enable the advanced security (pointing the browser to (https://account. live.com/proofs/Manage), as follows:

1. First, we are prompted with a security check, the confirmation of the alternative e-mail address, and the input of a verification code.

Think about it; what is the most important aspect of an account that you need to protect? If a user changes the security information (such as the alternative e-mail address, personal information, and access details) the actual owner would forever lose access to the account. In fact, the first thing a malicious user is going to do is to enter an account and change its password, so as to block the rightful user out of it.

2. After entering the code, we can set up the advanced security, by adding:

   ° **An alternative verification method (additional to the alternative e-mail address)**: This could be a mobile phone number, which is capable of receiving SMSs with verification codes.

   ° **Alerting options**: In case of suspicious activity, we can receive an alert on the alternative contact details (e-mail addresses and/or mobile phone numbers).

- ° **Recovery code**: This is a *product-key-like* code to keep the account isolated, and can give access to it in various cases (such as forgotten passwords and compromised security).

- ° **Two-step verification**: This is probably the most effective and secure option to protect a Microsoft account. It enables authentication by adding a two-step verification layer.

3. Once you implement one (or all) of the preceding security measures, a Microsoft account is definitely safer than before, since now the authentication requires something that *we know* and *have*.

Let's explore the two-step verification a little bit in detail.

 Since the two-step verification could be an overkill for ordinary e-mail usage, it is convenient to create a Microsoft account for the management purposes of Azure only, and then enable the advanced security on it.

Two-step verification

The two-step verification can be turned on in the **Protect your account** page (refer to `https://account.live.com/proofs/Manage`). After turning it on, we are asked for an additional verification (the same used while trying to access the security information) on each login. In addition to this, for each application that cannot accept a **Two-step verification** workflow, we need to create an app password:

Two-step verification

Two-step verification is an advanced security feature that makes it harder for a hacker to sign in to your account with just a stolen password. Learn more about whether this is right for you.

Set up two-step verification

This is the area where we can enable the two-step verification

App passwords are random strings used to link remote applications with the Microsoft account, without compromising the main security information, that is, the main password. The following figure shows a window where we can set up app passwords:

App passwords

Some apps and devices (such as Xbox 360, Windows Phone, or mail apps on your other devices) don't support security codes for two-step verification. In these cases, you need to create an app password to sign in. Learn more about app passwords.

Create a new app password

Remove existing app passwords

With app passwords, we can at any time revoke the right that a remote app has to access the account centrally, and without changing the main password.

Authenticator app

There are two common ways to implement the two-step verification:

- Mobile phones (SMS)
- E-mail verifications

However, how is it possible to access the alternative e-mail when there is no GSM coverage to receive the code via SMS?

In the advanced security section of the Microsoft account website, we can also enable the **Identity verification apps** workflow. As we can see in the following figure, we can set up a smartphone to act as a security token generator, similar to many online banking systems:

Identity verification apps

A smartphone app is the fastest way to verify your identity. Learn more.

Set up

Once the application (available for Windows and Android phones) is installed and correctly set up (through the website), a symmetric token is maintained on both sides (on Microsoft and the smartphone) through a time-based algorithm, plus a key. This ensures that, in the case of isolation on the smartphone, the codes are correct.

Security Paranoia: Is smartphone verification safe?

While enforcing IT security, each link between the involved parties should be secure. It means that it is not secure by itself using a smartphone to authenticate (or verify). If the smartphone is not secured as well, from the hacker's perspective, it is just one more step which can be used to break the account. Thus, it is important to enforce security on the smartphone also, by enabling a lock screen with a PIN (or password), to prevent random users from accessing applications and, of course, the verification methods used.

As we saw in the previous chapter, security is not a combination of tools and complex words, but a checklist of best practices and processes to be implemented to guarantee the highest protection available. Imagine a two-step verification using a code via SMS: is this secure just because it involves a personal device? In many cases, the answer is *yes*, but if the malicious user is in the same room as the account owner, he or she can easily gain access to the device and check for the verification code. This is why it is important to lock the device properly (as we probably already do with our laptop/computer when we are not using it).

Finally, in modern smartphones where notifications appear on the top section of the screen (even when the screen is locked), a code is sent by SMS or a push notification can be easily taken without unlocking the device, so *be aware* of this.

IAM in the Preview portal

The Preview portal, which you can refer to at `https://portal.azure.com`, is accessible with a valid credential, such as a Microsoft account or a company account (hosted on Azure AD). Discussing the new features of this portal is out of the scope of this book but, from an IT and security perspective, great features have been added to it.

A completely renewed role-based authorization engine is implemented to set up fine grained security for each component of the platform, as we can see in the next section.

At the time of writing this book, there are some limitations in the Preview portal; not every Azure service is available to be managed and not all the features of available services are aligned with the current portal.

Role-Based Access Control

Users have been demanding this feature for a long time and, finally, it has arrived. In the Preview portal, the *old* users (such as the service administrator and the co-administrators) are grouped in the cumulative user, **Subscription admins**, with the default role of the **Owner**, which is the highest level of permission set made available.

This is done to provide backward compatibility with the current portal, as well as to let existing administrators continue to operate the entire subscription. However, since there is a fine grained authorization engine in place now, new accesses should be granted properly.

Roles

There are three roles currently available in the portal:

- **Owner**: The owner can manage everything, including access
- **Contributor**: The contributor can manage everything, except access
- **Reader**: The reader can view everything, but they cannot make changes

A user can be placed into one (or more) of these roles, as performed in most of the role-based authorization engines.

 A user can be, as we have seen before, a valid Microsoft account or an existing user (or security group) of the Azure AD of the subscription.

Microsoft stated that in an upcoming release of RBAC, administrators of Azure accounts could define custom roles by composing a set of actions from a list of the ones available that can be performed on Azure resources (refer to `http://azure.microsoft.com/en-us/documentation/articles/role-based-access-control-configure/`).

Hierarchy of security objects

In file-system security, we are confident that in case of assigning a "full control" permission to a given user for given folders, all the subfolders (with default settings) inherit the same permission set too. In the Preview portal, the hierarchy is as follows:

- **Subscription**: The permission given at the subscription level is valid for each object within the subscription (that is, a **Reader** subscription can view everything within the same subscription).

- **Resource group**: This is a fairly new concept in Azure. A **resource group** is (as the name suggests) a group or resources which are logically connected, as the collection of resources for the same web project (a web hosting plan, SQL Server, and so on). A permission given at this level is valid for each object within the resource group.

- **Individual resource**: The permission given to an individual resource is valid only for this particular resource (that is, giving read-only access to a client to the Application Insights of a Website).

> We need to clarify that an individual resource is a service-level object (such as a storage account, Website and an SQL database) and not an individual object inside some services (such as a Blob, page, table). This can sound trivial but it is necessary to avoid confusion.

Adding a user in the Preview portal

Managing authentication/authorization in the Preview portal is pretty easy and straightforward. In the following example, we can see how to add two users (one internal, and the other external) to a subscription:

1. Go to the Preview portal at `https://portal.azure.com`.

2. In the **BROWSE** item menu on the left, select **Subscriptions**.

3. Select **Subscription** to manage; a new detail area will appear.

4. In the **Access** group, select the **Users** part, a new detail area will appear, where the existing users are shown:

5. Click on the **Add** button on the menu on top.

6. Select the **Contributor** role and from the list of users in the directory, select the user(s) you want to add and confirm. Add a user from its Microsoft account.

7. Select the **Reader** role and then click on **Invite** in the upper menu.

8. Enter the Microsoft account address and confirm it.

An example of an authorization panel is shown in this figure:

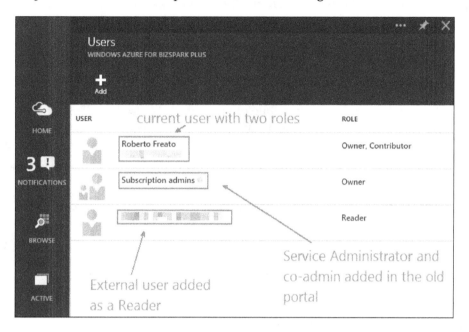

There is an external user known as **Owner** + **Contributor** (it is redundant since the permission of the **Owner** wins over the **Contributor** ones); the **Subscription admins** are created by default and an external user is added as the **Reader** of the entire subscription.

Advanced authentication

In this section, we will see two advanced scenarios used to authenticate against Azure services. The first is the **Multi-Factor Authentication**, which is useful to secure the directory users' accounts with a two-step verification; the second are **Management Certificates**, used to establish a secure channel between two parties and operate as administrators against a given subscription.

Multi-Factor Authentication

Azure AD has built-in features to enable Multi-Factor Authentication for its users. As for the two-step verification of the Microsoft account (discussed earlier in the chapter) Multi-Factor Authentication involves more than just one *factor*, combining:

- **What we know**: This refers to valid credentials
- **What we have**: This refers to a device, for example

In Azure AD, we have these options:

- **Authentication apps** for mobile phones, available for Windows Phone, Android, and iOS. With the authentication app, users can receive one-time passcodes via push notifications or generate them from the application itself.
- **Automated phone calls** that, once received, have to be answered and the user has to press # to confirm authentication.
- **Automated SMS messages** containing the one-time passcode.

These are the links to the various Authentication apps:

Windows Phone: You can refer to `http://www.windowsphone.com/en-us/store/app/multi-factor-auth/0a9691de-c0a1-44ee-ab96-6807f8322bd1`.

Android: You can refer to `https://play.google.com/store/apps/details?id=com.phonefactor.phonefactor&feature=search_result`.

iOS: You can refer to `https://itunes.apple.com/us/app/phonefactor/id475844606?mt=8`.

Setting up Multi-Factor Authentication

Administrators can set up Multi-Factor Authentication for their users from the Azure current portal, as follows:

1. Go to the **USERS** tab of the selected Azure AD.
2. On the bottom menu, click on the **MANAGE MULTI-FACTOR AUTH** button.
3. Once you are redirected to an another website (refer to `https://account.activedirectory.windowsazure.com`) select the users to enable.
4. In the **quick steps** menu on the right-hand side of the page, click on **Enable.**

5. Set up the Multi-Factor Authentication for the user.

6. Open a new browser window and point to `https://account.activedirectory.windowsazure.com`.

 Using the incognito mode for Chrome, or the InPrivate mode for IE, is better while working with multiple credentials.

7. Enter the username and the password for the given user; a screen like this one should appear:

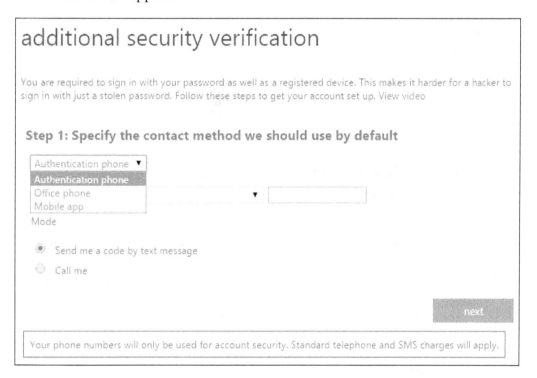

8. Enter the intended validation mode (that is, **Mobile app**)

9. Download the **Mobile app** to the smartphone and complete the pairing process:

   ° Enter pairing codes or scan a QR to pair

   ° Verify the connection

   ° Enter the alternative phone number

10. Try to authenticate again with the Azure AD credentials. A push notification will appear asking you to confirm to continue. Now, all is set.

 For advanced features related to Multi-Factor Authentication, see the Multi-Factor Authentication Provider feature at `http://technet.microsoft.com/en-us/library/dn376348.aspx`.

Management Certificates

Management Certificates are useful to set up a trust between a third party and the Azure Platform. A Management Certificate is created by the administrator (or by a co-administrator) and uploaded to the current portal. Consequently, the private key holder (an automated client, for example) can authenticate to the platform and operate with administrator privileges. In the book, *Microsoft Azure Development Cookbook Second Edition*, *Packt Publishing*, there is an entire chapter about automating the Azure Management through C# and the Management API, which relies on certificates to work. An excerpt of this chapter is given in the next section, showing you how to create and set up a Management Certificate.

Setting up a Management Certificate

To create a self-signed X509 certificate on the local machine and upload it to Azure, proceed as follows:

1. Open a Developer Command Prompt and go to a local folder where the certificate's public key is stored.

2. Run the following command, replacing `CertificateName` with real values:

```
makecert -sky exchange -r -n "CN=<CertificateName>" -pe -a
   sha1 -len 2048 -ss My "<CertificateName>.cer"
```

3. After this:

   ° In the current folder, a `.cer` file is created

   ° In the local user store, a complete certificate is saved

To make the entire certificate (including its private key) portable, follow these steps:

1. Press Windows + *R* (the `run` command) and run mmc.

2. Navigate to **File | Add/Remove Snap-in...** and select **Certificates** (my user account).

3. Once you have navigated to the **Personal | Certificates** folder, find the certificate created previously (it will show as `CertificateName`, according to the one specified previously).

4. Right-click on it, then navigate to **All Tasks | Export** and follow the wizard to export a **Personal Information Exchange** (**PFX**) file wherever convenient (select **Yes**, export the private key, and specify a good password).

To create the trust between Azure and our certificate, upload the public key to the portal, as follows:

1. Go to the **Azure Portal** and locate the **MANAGEMENT CERTIFICATES** tab in the **SETTINGS** section.

2. In menu at the bottom, click on **Upload** and upload the previously created `.cer` file.

Once completed, a trust is established and the holder of the private key can operate against Azure through the Management API.

 Be careful: Sometimes Visual Studio and other software automatically create Management Certificates. Know your certificates and revoke them if not necessary anymore.

Summary

In this chapter, we highlighted the importance of securing the account used to access Azure resources. We used the Microsoft account with the two-step verification, used Azure AD, and we implemented a Multi-Factor Authentication that, in conjunction with RBAC, can put the Azure administration inside a good security boundary.

In the next chapter, we talk about *Platform as a Service*. By discussing some of the PaaS services of Azure, we will highlight how to use them properly and focus on the security issues they are related to.

3
Platform as a Service

Microsoft Azure is a Cloud computing platform, offering various services from **Infrastructure as a Service (IaaS)** to SaaS, and finally to PaaS. My personal opinion is that PaaS is the future (but also the present) of what exactly Cloud computing should mean to us: using ready-to-go platforms without too much specific expertise, focusing on *what we need to run* and not on *how to run* it.

However, not every scenario is compatible with PaaS, so it is not uncommon to mix some good PaaS with IaaS (as in a recipe). In this chapter, we are going to discuss the most important Azure PaaS building blocks and highlight the security aspects of:

- Websites and Cloud Services
- Storage and SQL Database
- Cache and Service Bus

The purpose of this chapter is to highlight the best practices used in terms of security, while using Azure PaaS, with no specific in-depth details about application security.

Hosting the code

Although there are several ways to host a custom code on Azure, the two most important building blocks are Websites and Cloud Services. The first is actually a PaaS built on top of the second (a PaaS too), using an open source engine named Project Kudu (refer to `https://github.com/projectkudu/kudu`). This is why we start by inspecting Cloud Services first.

Cloud Services

Cloud Services was the first Azure Service that came out in the early stages of the platform (in 2009). In this book, it is assumed that you are familiar with Azure Services; however, here is a quick recap of some of the key concepts when working with Cloud Services:

1. Write the application.
2. Wrap it in a specific artifact named `Cloud Service`.

    ° Configure it with configuration files

3. Package the code and configuration with specific tools.
4. Upload to Azure and let it create the environment to run the application.

 A complete guide on Cloud Services, including step-by-step examples, can be looked up in my other book, *Microsoft Azure Development Cookbook Second Edition, Packt Publishing*, available at `https://www.packtpub.com/application-development/microsoft-azure-development-cookbook-second-edition`.

From the security perspective, we are going to inspect these aspects:

*   Remote endpoints
*   Remote Desktop
*   Startup tasks
*   Microsoft Antimalware
*   Network communication

Remote endpoints

An Azure Cloud Service is a container of roles. A **role** is the representation of a unit of execution and it can be a **worker role** (an arbitrary application) or a **web role** (an IIS application). Each role within a Cloud Service can be deployed to several VMs (instances) at the same time, to provide scalability and load-balancing, as in the following figure:

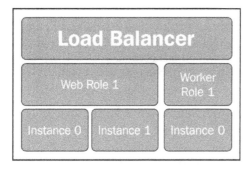

Before deployment, the definition of the service and the code for the various roles has to be packaged into a single `.cspkg` file. Along with that, a `.cscfg` file (a service configuration) is required to provide actual configuration values to the definition of the Cloud Service.

Although you can actually deploy a Cloud Service with no open public endpoints, in case of web roles, you would probably do that in order to let remote users connect to the web services of your role; instead, a worker role can be deployed without active endpoints, except for the cases where it actively listens for network communication. To be sure that only the necessary endpoints are opened in the roles, we can check this section of the service definition:

```
      </Bindings>
    </Site>
  </Sites>
  <Endpoints>                                              +
    <InputEndpoint name="Endpoint1" protocol="http" port="80" />
  </Endpoints>
</WebRole>
```

We can also check the **Configuration** page of the role:

Please remember that this is the actual configuration of the firewall rules of the load balancer. If the application opens a TCP endpoint listening for incoming connections, no connections will be established if the load balancer does not have the appropriate rules.

Remote Desktop

I prefer to consider Cloud Services as collections of roles/instances acting as black boxes, where the input is the *application* and the output is the *work and logs*. However, we can (but shouldn't, in my opinion) connect to the actual VM instances to get some information or perform debugging, especially during the development and testing phases. To achieve this, with regard to what is mentioned in the previous section, an **Input** endpoint is required. To avoid configuration errors or repetition, Azure introduces the concept of extensions. An **extension** is a module pluggable in the Cloud Service that enables a specific service. The Remote Desktop module, when set appropriately through Visual Studio or the Azure Management Portal, automatically adds to the balancer of the firewall exception for the **Remote Desktop Protocol (RDP)** service. In addition to this, it configures each instance of the given service with the appropriate RDP configuration and credentials.

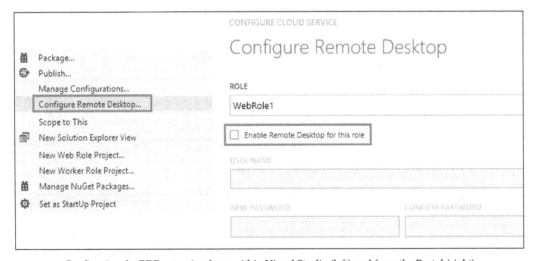

Configuring the RDP extension from within Visual Studio (left) and from the Portal (right)

Despite the fact that the credentials are encrypted (through certificates) in the service configuration file and the communication between the user and the remote instances is also encrypted, running production workloads with RDP enabled is not recommended.

VM used in Cloud Services are to be intended for stateless use, since the code and configuration should come with the deployment (service package, configuration, and startup tasks). There shouldn't be a need to open RDP on such instances.

Furthermore, the Remote Desktop module also enables the capability to perform incremental updates of the running code in roles, using **Web Deploy**.

As per the MSDN documentation (refer to `https://msdn.microsoft.com/en-us/library/azure/ff683672.aspx`):

This is required so that Web Deploy can use the user and password to connect to the virtual machine to deploy the changes to the server that's running Internet Information Services (IIS).

Web Deploy can be enabled during deployment, as in the following figure:

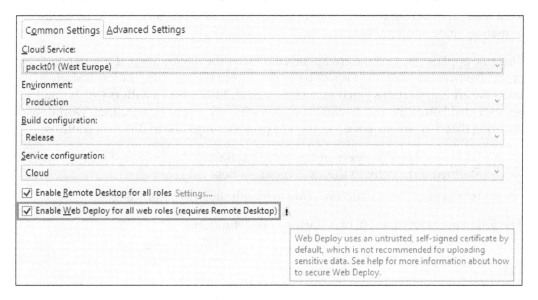

Enabling Web Deploy may be useful; however, it is not recommended that you use it in production because:

- Web Deploy uses an untrusted, self-signed certificate, by default
- Changes are made only to the running code in case of recycling (or re-imaging) the changes are lost and they have to be republished

The **re-image process** is the process of recreation of a new VM, based on the service package provided during the last complete deployment. This is particularly useful when the instance is somehow compromised.

- It supports only web roles with one instance only

Startup tasks

Cloud Services are sets of roles/instances where application code can run. These instances must be treated as stateless because, in certain circumstances, Azure can recycle a VM. In this case, any data generated between the deployment of the service package and recycling can be lost.

Most distributed environments are designed around the *stateless* concept. When developers design applications, they should avoid using any transient storage or local data repositories. Instead, a central, externalized repository should be used to manage state and application data.

This rule applies also to the software installed after the deployment: if it is not part of the deployment itself, then it will be lost as part of the recycling process. **Startup tasks** are arbitrary actions (such as custom scripts, **Microsoft Installers** (**MSIs**), and so on) executed before the role begins. They comply with a specific execution workflow, ensuring that they are processed at the VM provisioning time in different contexts:

- `limited`: The privileges of the startup tasks are the same as the role, except defined differently in the `<Runtime>` section
- `elevated`: The startup task runs with administrative privileges

The following is an example of a startup task definition:

```
<Runtime executionContext="limited">
</Runtime>
<Startup>
  <Task taskType="simple" executionContext="elevated" commandLine="command.cmd">
    <Environment>
      <Variable name="MySetting" value="MyValue" />
    </Environment>
  </Task>
</Startup>
```

Startup tasks running with administrative privileges may perform some actions on the IIS configuration or may install some custom tool that can compromise security and create vulnerabilities. As they are arbitrary processes, limiting their privileges to the minimum is a good practice.

Microsoft Antimalware

The **Antimalware** module is an Azure extension available for both Cloud Services and VMs.

 Extensions are pluggable modules inside a given Azure VM, so they can introduce vulnerabilities; however, in this case, this extension is supposed to give some more protection to the running system.

With Cloud Services, the Antimalware service is installed and disabled by default in each role, and it can be enabled from the Azure Portal or via PowerShell, providing:

- **Real-time protection**: It continuously monitors running programs to detect and block malware
- **Scheduled quick/full scanning**: It scans the entire system on a scheduled basis, with exclusions, if provided
- **Engine/platform/definition auto-update**: It automatically gets updates from Microsoft Download Center

To verify the status of the Antimalware extension for a given Cloud Service, we can use this PowerShell walkthrough:

1. Download the Azure PowerShell and start it.
2. Use the `Add-AzureAccount` cmdlets to link your subscription to the session.
3. Use the `Get-AzureSubscription` cmdlets to list all the available subscriptions.
4. Use the `Select-AzureSubscription "[subscription]"` cmdlets to operate on the desired subscription.
5. Use the `Get-AzureServiceAntimalwareConfig "[cloudService]"` cmdlets to obtain the extension configuration.

If the Antimalware extension is installed, the following XML configuration snippet should be available:

```
<AntimalwareConfig xmlns:xsd="http://www.w3.org/2001/XMLSchema"
  xmlns:xsi="http://www.w3.org/2001/XMLSchema-instance">
  <AntimalwareEnabled>true</AntimalwareEnabled>
  <RealtimeProtectionEnabled>true</RealtimeProtectionEnabled>
  <ScheduledScanSettings isEnabled="true" day="7" time="120"
  scanType="Full" />
</AntimalwareConfig>
```

If not, we can enable it with the following snippet:

```
$XmlConfig = New-Object System.Xml.XmlDocument
$XmlConfig.load('path to a valid config XML')
Set-AzureServiceAntimalwareExtension -ServiceName "MyCloudService"
  -Slot "Staging" -AntimalwareConfiguration $XmlConfig
```

The specifications for the XML file can be found at `http://msdn.microsoft.com/en-us/library/azure/dn771718.aspx`.

Network communication

Cloud Services are provided by default with a **load balancer** that also acts as a firewall for incoming connections. We see, in the *Remote endpoints* section, that an instance can be reached from outside Azure, only through one Input endpoint defined in the service definition and, consequently, opened on the load balancer side.

However, if the various roles/instances of a given service need to communicate with each other, a more convenient way is to set up an Internal endpoint. **Internal endpoints** are, as the name suggests, TCP/IP endpoints, opened on the VMs, accessible only from within the VMs subnet of the Cloud Service itself. Consequently, nobody from the Internet can access these endpoints from outside the deployment, making it the preferred way to let instances communicate with each other. In addition to this, the segment of networks where the VMs communicate is isolated from other Azure customers, providing a more secure environment for services.

We can define an endpoint directly from Visual Studio, as follows:

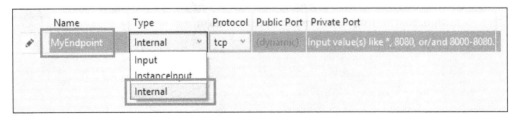

After this, from a C#.NET application, the internal endpoints can be discovered through the `RoleEnvironment` **Application Program Interface (API)**, as follows:

```
IEnumerable<IPEndPoint> endpoints =
  RoleEnvironment.Roles["WebRole1"]
  .Instances.Select(p => p.InstanceEndpoints
  ["MyEndpoint"].IPEndpoint);
```

The preceding snippet asks for the Internal endpoint defined as `MyEndpoint`, for a given role (`WebRole1`), for each running instance it finds.

As we can see in the preceding screenshot, another type of endpoint is available; **InstanceInput endpoint** is an endpoint that maps a given load balancer port range to specific instances, as follows:

```
<WorkerRole name="WorkerRole1" vmsize="Small">
  <Endpoints>
    <InstanceInputEndpoint name="MyEndpoint" protocol="tcp" localPort="10100">
      <AllocatePublicPortFrom>
        <FixedPortRange max="10104" min="10100" />
      </AllocatePublicPortFrom>
    </InstanceInputEndpoint>
  </Endpoints>
</WorkerRole>
```

This `InstanceInputEndpoint` defines a port range of 5 public ports to the port `10100`, of up to five instances of `WorkerRole1`. Since this feature exposes the individual VM of a given role to direct Internet access, this could lead to security issues. As for the Remote Desktop feature, it gives much more control over the deployment, but I would not rely on it for production workloads.

Websites

Azure **Websites** are some of the most advanced PaaS in the Cloud computing market, providing users with a lock-in free solution to run applications built in various languages/platforms. Assuming at we use the standard pricing mode, the running model is pretty straightforward:

- A user creates a web hosting plan, defining the size and the number of VMs to allocate (or defining an autoscale policy)

- A user creates one or more Websites in a given web hosting plan, which will run all of them together in the same VM pool, isolated between each other

To confirm what we just expressed, this is a simple diagram explaining the infrastructure:

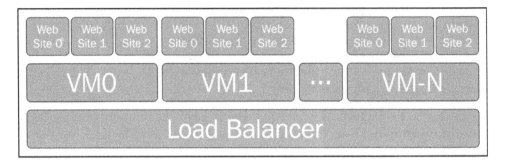

The load balancer is configured to reply on the various DNS names of the actual websites deployed in the VMs, redirecting the traffic based on a simple round-robin algorithm. In addition to this, it is possible to enable **sticky sessions** on the load balancer that runs the **Application Request Routing** (**ARR**) for IIS extensions, setting a default **affinity cookie** to each request, making consecutive calls from the same client going to the same VM.

Other than in Cloud Services, where the minimum count for instances to have the SLA is two, in Websites there is no such constraint. In the **BASIC** and **STANDARD** modes, the SLA applies even to a single instance (no SLA is provided with **FREE** or **SHARED** modes).

Before inspecting the various security aspects of Azure Websites, we need to know a little about the engine that makes this glue between IIS and the actual web applications, since it is an open source project named Project Kudu; after that, we can look at:

- Credentials
- Connection modes
- Settings and connection strings
- Backups
- Extensions

The POODLE issue: In 2014, a serious vulnerability in the SSL 3.0 protocol implementation was found. The **POODLE** (short for **Padding Oracle On Downgraded Legacy Encryption**) attack allowed the stealing of HTTP cookies or bearer tokens with sensitive information (like authorization headers). Microsoft released a bulletin with more information about this vulnerability at `https://technet.microsoft.com/en-us/library/security/3009008.aspx`. The POODLE issue is not related to a specific product or service of Microsoft, but it involves implementation of the entire SSL 3.0 version. Websites, as managed services, have been updated to disable the affected protocol in favor of more recent and secure implementations (TLS protocols).

Project Kudu

Kudu is an open source engine working with IIS, which manages automatic or manual deployments of Azure Websites in a sandboxed environment. Kudu can also run outside Azure, but it is primarily supported to enable Website services.

Kudu is not a multi-tenant engine: this means that in case of multiple websites in a given VM (circumstances are anything but rare), multiple Kudu instances will run. Each instance of the Kudu service runs in a sandboxed environment, with a limited set of privileges, having sufficient access to the website data only. However, Kudu is also the name of the *administration* site of the website itself. If a user creates a `[newsite].azurewebsites.net` website, the Kudu site will run on `[newsite].scm.azurewebsites.net`, whose access is protected with appropriate credentials. Kudu services can harm the environment where they run, leaving the other components of the operating systems untouched.

As Kudu runs in a sandboxed environment with limited privileges, only the *normal* operation of websites is allowed. This means that access to operating system files is restricted, and so is the access to other Kudu instances or the Socket API (no, we cannot open a listening Socket).

Credentials

For a given Azure Website, typically two types of credentials are available:

- User-level credentials
- Site-level credentials

User-level credentials are related to a user that manages the Azure assets. If a Microsoft account (or Azure AD account) is added as a co-administrator to a subscription, or has at least the contributor's permission to a website, it can configure a set of credentials valid for every Azure Website, which is somehow linked to this account. The user-level credentials can be configured in the current portal:

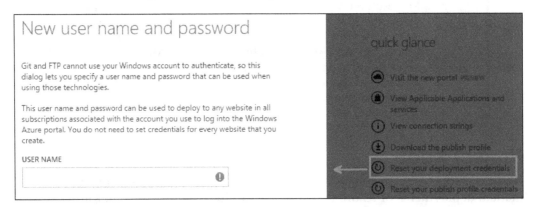

Similarly, in the new portal, the credentials can be set as per this image:

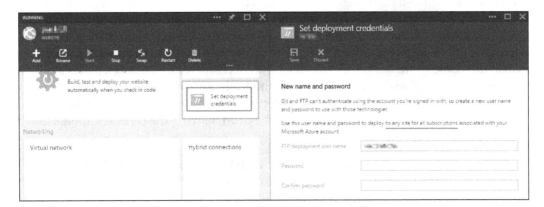

 Note that with user-level credentials, the FTP connection username must be in the form applicable, that is, [nameOfTheSite]\[chosenUsername].

Site-level credentials are, instead, the credentials contained on the site-level published profile. While user-level credentials are often human-readable (and they can be memorized), site-level credentials always follow this pattern:

- **Web deploy username**: This refers to $[nameOfTheSite].

- **FTP username**: This refers to [nameOfTheSite]\$[nameOfTheSite].

- **Password**: It's the same for both types of access. It is a random string of about 60 characters.

This is an example of a publish profile with the Web Deploy and FTP settings:

```xml
<?xml version="1.0"?>
<publishData>
  <publishProfile profileName="Root" publishMethod="MSDeploy"
  publishUrl="[site].scm.azurewebsites.net:443"
  msdeploySite="[site]" userName="$[site]" userPWD="[userPWD]"
  destinationAppUrl="http://[site].azurewebsites.net"
  SQLServerDBConnectionString="" mySQLDBConnectionString=""
  hostingProviderForumLink=""
  controlPanelLink="http://windows.azure.com"
  webSystem="WebSites">
    <databases/>
    <publishProfile profileName="FTP" publishMethod="FTP"
    publishUrl="ftp://[pool].ftp.azurewebsites.windows.
    net/site/wwwroot" ftpPassiveMode="True"
    userName="[site]\$[site]" userPWD="[userPWD]"
    destinationAppUrl="http://[site].azurewebsites.net"
    SQLServerDBConnectionString="" mySQLDBConnectionString=""
    hostingProviderForumLink=""
    controlPanelLink="http://windows.azure.com"
    webSystem="WebSites">
    <databases/>
  </publishProfile>
</publishData>
```

Publish profile is the key entry point for a website's security, embedding all the information to publish (and also destroy) the content of an Azure Website. It is recommended that you keep it in a safe place and, in case of leaks, it can be regenerated from the Management Portal.

> While publishing a website from Visual Studio, if a published profile is supplied, Visual Studio saves the basic endpoint information (plus the publishing username) in the `Properties/PublishProfiles` project folder. The password, however, is saved and encrypted, to avoid unintentional disclosures through a source control system or in some other way.

Connection modes

Azure Websites can be deployed from any Git repository (that is, in fact, the purpose of Project Kudu itself) through several providers of automated deployment (such as Visual Studio Online, CodePlex, GitHub, Dropbox, and so on), but also through two *manual* methods: FTP and Web Deploy.

FTP is very simple and compatible with almost every scenario. An Azure Website offers a **TLS** (short for **Transport Layer Security**)-secure FTP endpoint, accessible with either a user-level credential or a site-level one. Web Deploy, instead, is definitely a great bang for your buck since:

- It is HTTPS based, so it is usually accessible through port 443, which is opened in most firewall configurations
- It performs incremental updates, publishing only those files that have changed since the last publishing
- It is configurable to deploy databases and perform additional actions

Though both Visual Studio and WebMatrix are able to automatically detect the Web Deploy endpoint from a published profile, the endpoint pattern is this (for reference purposes only):

```
[nameOfTheSite].scm.azurewebsites.net:443
```

As previously mentioned, it is always recommended to use the site-level credentials for both FTP and Web Deploy, since they can be regenerated on a site-by-site basis.

Settings and connection strings

Developers often embed their sensitive information in the source code by writing it down in the configuration files. In the .NET world, the web.config file is used in web applications to both store application settings and connection strings, as follows:

```xml
<configuration>
  <appSettings>
    <add key="MyKey" value="MyValueFromWebConfig"/>
  </appSettings>
  <connectionStrings>
    <add name="MyConnection" connectionString="MyValueFromWebConfig"/>
  </connectionStrings>
  <system.web>
```

Storing sensitive information, such as connection strings or application settings, is not recommended and should only be used for Dev/Test purposes. In addition to this, even if we use XML/XSLT transform (to replace debug settings with production ones while publishing) there is a concrete risk of making some mistakes while publishing and running the production code with Dev/Test settings (or pointing to a wrong database, for example).

With Websites, it is possible to avoid the following common security mistakes:

- Putting production/sensitive settings into the source code
- Making mistakes while publishing in production

In the Website management section of the **Azure Portal**, we can write down **app settings** and **connection strings** for the running solution, without affecting the existing behavior of the running application:

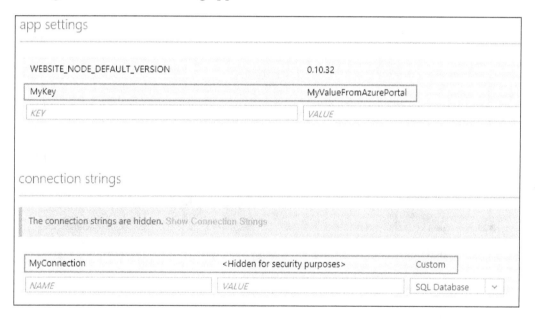

Actually, while asking for these settings, the application will read the portal-overridden settings, ignoring the ones written in the `web.config` (and related) files. This ensures that only the subscription administrator (or the one who has the rights to the Website, with RBAC) can read/manage the sensitive information.

Within the Management Portal, the connection strings have a name, value, and type. The type, at the time of writing this book, can be custom, SQL database, SQL Server, and MySQL, injecting the correct name in the `providerName` attribute of the actual connection string. However, with **Entity Framework (EF)**, things go wrong. This is because `providerName` for the EF connection string is `System.Data.EntityClient`, while it is `System.Data.SqlClient` if we choose the SQL database or SQL Server in the portal. To solve this issue, the workaround is:

- Write a connection string in the `web.config` with the correct `name` and `providerName`.
- Write an empty or default value for the `connectionString` attribute.
- Create an overriding connection string in the Management Portal, with the real value and the *Custom* type.

This will use `providerName` defined in `web.config`, while the `connectionString` value is taken from the Kudu engine.

Kudu automatically puts an environment variable for each setting specified in the **app settings** section, as shown in the following screenshot:

This is useful outside the .NET ecosystem; non-.NET languages and frameworks can also access these settings using existing skills, as follows (in PHP):

```php
test.php          ×
1  ⊟<?php
2    echo 'MyKey is ' .$_SERVER['MyKey'] . '!';
3    ?>
```

Navigating the **Environment** section of the Kudu administration site (such as `[siteName].scm.azurewebsites.net/Env`), we can also learn many environment variables available in the running application, for advanced scenarios.

Backups

A Website service has a native support for backups to a designated **Storage Account**. However, this section is not about the feature itself, but also on *how* Azure performs the backup and the associated security risks in this process:

These are the buttons to trigger Backup/Restore actions on a given website

To summarize the main security issue in a sentence: since the backup process backs up the content of the website and the entire configuration, a breach in the Storage Account where the backup is located affects the security of the entire website too.

Navigating through the **websitebackups** container of the Storage Account used for backups, we see two distinct files for each backup:

- `[siteName]_Date.zip`: This refers to the content of the root home, which includes everything Kudu needs to run the website
- `[siteName]_Date.xml`: This refers to a minimal configuration of the website

From a brief analysis of the XML configuration file, we can see that no sensitive information is directly exposed. However, this is not the X-file we are looking for. In the root of the ZIP archive, the `meta` file contains everything a malicious user would need to control the website, including:

- App settings
- Connection strings

- Publishing credentials (for FTP/Web Deploy)

 This is not the first case where we see that the security of an Azure Service depends on another's security measures. This can happen continuously, since it is common to mix services while designing Cloud solutions.

This is why it is so important to secure the Storage Account, where backups are located, at the highest possible security level.

Extensions

Extensions are a powerful feature of Azure Websites (and Kudu) that enable advanced scenarios of manipulating the content of the site or the `ApplicationHost.config` file. There are two types of extensions:

- **Native (or preinstalled)**: These are available for all sites. The Kudu administration site living on the `[siteName].scm.azurewebsites.net` URL is an example of an extension. Also, *Monaco* (a Visual Studio Online editor), is usable as a site extension.
- **Third-party (private or from a gallery)**: These are installed by the user to a specific website.

From a security point of view, an extension has the permissions to apply **XML Document Transformation** (**XDT**) to the `ApplicationHost.config` file by adding:

- New applications on the **Source Control Manager** (**SCM**) site
- New applications on the main site
- Modules and other changes to the ASP.NET pipeline

Running with the same permissions set as on a website, an extension can also manipulate the website's file-system to perform additional actions:

- Create web jobs
- Modify the content files of a website

Additional resources about site extensions are available at: `https://github.com/projectkudu/kudu/wiki/Azure-Site-Extensions`.

Hosting the data

Azure Services have grown faster (as in the number of services and the surface area) than in the past, at an amazingly increasing rate, and consequently, we have several options to store any kind of data (such as relational, NoSQL, binary, JSON, and so on), but in this part we focus on the two main services we've found since the beginning of Azure: Storage and the SQL database (the former known as *SQL Azure*).

Storage

Azure Storage is the base service for almost everything on the platform: VMs use it explicitly to host the disks. Cloud Services use it transparently for the same purpose, users take advantage of it to store application data, and almost every service uses it to save diagnostic and logging data.

Storage security is implemented in two different ways:

- Account keys
- Shared Access Signatures

Account keys

When a Storage Account is created, two Account keys (primary and secondary) provide full access to the various services of the Storage Account (blobs, tables, queues, and files). It is of vital importance that these keys are kept safe to avoid loss of confidentiality, integrity, or availability:

This is where we can obtain/copy and re-generate the Access Keys for a Storage Account

A malicious user with access to a Storage Account Key can:

- Create new data, generating costs
- Download existing data, breaking confidentiality
- Edit existing data, which can lead to an integrity issue (but also availability) and application errors

 If an application, in fact, relies on something in a particular form, hosted in the Storage Account, any modification can break the contract, generating a runtime error. In addition to this, a storage service does not have a backup/restore solution bundled, except for the one performed transparently by Microsoft for disaster recovery.

Storage Account Keys come in pairs to encourage rotation while preserving availability. This is illustrated with the following example.

At a given time, T, a company has several web applications deployed using the primary Storage Account Key. However, we are sure that the key has been disclosed and we need to change it without service interruption. With a secondary key, we can replace the old primary one with a secondary in every running web application. After this, we can regenerate the primary one to leave out malicious users.

 Note that changing a key for a given Storage Account will also invalidate every Shared Access Signature generated with this key.

The key rotation has no impact on other Azure Services linked to the Storage Account, such as Website diagnostics, SQL Database Automated Export, and so on. In these cases, the configuration is performed at the subscription's administrator level, referencing just the Storage Account without the corresponding access key.

Some general advice while using Azure Storage is to minimally reduce the parties owning the access keys, encouraging the use of Shared Access Signatures, as we will see in the following section.

Shared Access Signatures

A **Shared Access Signature** (**SAS**) is a fine-grained and powerful way to grant permission to a storage object (a blob, table, or queue) without disclosing the Account key.

The key points are:

- The resource to share
- The time frame validity of the permission
- The type of permission

Based on this information and an Access Key, a signature is generated. A typical SAS URL for a given Blob is given as `https://[account].blob.core.windows.net/[container]/[blob]?sr=b&sv=2014-02-14&st=2014-12-24T15%3A54%3A25Z&se=2014-12-24T16%3A54%3A25Z&sp=r&sig=g08Y2bRFZQDBT7bEFxPJldAs9WEYOHTWrCnOcR3cqe8%3D`.

This URL is valid while the Account key that generated it is still valid. Upon regeneration, the SAS must be regenerated as well. Note that the only way to revoke a SAS is to regenerate the Account key, which may have other serious implications. A SAS can be generated through the portal or by code, as follows:

```
CloudBlockBlob cloudBlockBlob = null; //suppose we have it
SharedAccessBlobPolicy sharedAccessPolicy =
  new SharedAccessBlobPolicy()
  {
    Permissions = SharedAccessBlobPermissions.Read,
    SharedAccessStartTime =
    DateTime.UtcNow.AddDays(-2),
    SharedAccessExpiryTime =
    DateTime.UtcNow.AddDays(2)
  };
var sharedAccessSignature =
  cloudBlockBlob.GetSharedAccessSignature(sharedAccessPolicy);
```

This SAS, if appended to the fully qualified URL of the blob, enables *read* access to the given blob for a period of two days to anonymous users.

Another option is to use Stored Access Policy: a policy is a definition of a permission with a validity period, which is applied to arbitrary resources. A typical SAS URL for a given Blob, using the Stored Access Policy named `Test` is given as `https://[account].blob.core.windows.net/[container]/[blob]?sr=b&sv=2014-02-14&si=Test&sig=UXMWXGW9V7QHXgO2BnqMlH9j12zudwoccw64QJEQmkY%3D`.

You may notice that Start time (`st`), End time (`se`) and Permission (`sp`) are missing. We just reference the `Test` policy (`si` parameter), instead. In this scenario, revoking access is simpler, since it is only necessary to remove or change the `Test` policy.

Even SAPs can be created by code, as follows:

```
CloudBlobContainer container = null; //Suppose we have it
DateTime startTime = DateTime.UtcNow;
SharedAccessBlobPolicy sharedAccessPolicy =
  new SharedAccessBlobPolicy()
  {
    Permissions = SharedAccessBlobPermissions.Read |
    SharedAccessBlobPermissions.Write,
    SharedAccessStartTime = startTime,
    SharedAccessExpiryTime = startTime.AddDays(3d)
  };

BlobContainerPermissions blobContainerPermissions =
  new BlobContainerPermissions();
blobContainerPermissions.SharedAccessPolicies.Add(
  "myPolicy", sharedAccessPolicy);

container.SetPermissions(blobContainerPermissions);
```

This policy is persisted into the Storage Account and it states that every SAS associated with it would have read/write access rights (for three days from the creation of the SAP) to every bit of content of the specified container.

A note about Storage Files: At the time of writing this book, Azure Storage Files is still in preview. **Storage Files** is a service, letting users create **SMB** (short for **Server Message Block**)-like network shares, to be mounted on Azure-hosted VMs, enabling many file-system-based scenarios. However, it is still not possible to use Storage Files with SAS, so we must keep an accurate track of parties using this feature, because they actually can control the whole account.

Scalability and performance targets

While looking at the specifications of many Azure Services, we often see the *scalability targets* section. For a given service, Azure provides users with a set of upper limits, in terms of capacity, bandwidth, and throughput to let them better design their Cloud solutions.

For reference purposes only, here is some scalability data about Storage Accounts in the US region (specifications are different in other regions):

- **Capacity**: 500 TB per Storage Account
- **Throughput**: 20000 request/sec

- **Bandwidth**: It is as follows:
  - ○ **Inbound**: It ranges from 10 Gbps to 20 Gbps
  - ○ **Outbound**: It ranges from 20 Gbps to 30 Gbps

We see that the bandwidth data shows a range. This is because we can have different pricing tiers and features. With the **Geo-Redundant Storage** (**GRS**), each object is replicated outside the region, and the corresponding bandwidth is lower; with the **Locally Redundant Storage** (**LRS**), each operation is replicated inside the region, with a remarkable gain of speed and bandwidth.

Each metric can also have security implications. For example:

- Is every actor, using the same Storage Account, relying on the maximum space?
- Are we sharing the same Storage Account with diagnostics and logging service?
- Are we exposing the Storage Account to the end users (for static web contents) with the expected concurrent requests more than the maximum throughput?
- Are the users (even a few) downloading huge files continuously?

These are some simple questions that can help while architecting a scalable solution. For a more complete reference, you may refer to `http://msdn.microsoft.com/en-us/library/azure/dn249410.aspx`.

SQL Database

Depending on the specific storage needs, Azure has a corresponding product/ service. If we need to save binary files, there is a `Blob` service in the Azure Storage; if we need to save a JSON document, we will probably use the `DocumentDB` service; finally, if we need relational, we have SQL Database.

From a developer's perspective, SQL Database is like a plain SQL Server endpoint, except for some features which are not available; a developer can connect to a SQL Database using the same techniques and technologies as previously done with SQL Server.

Working with SQL Database is straightforward. However, a few best practices must be implemented to improve security:

- Setting up firewall rules
- Setting up users and roles
- Connection settings

Custom backup/replication solutions are not in the scope of this book, since the recent versions of SQL Database (basic, standard or premium) provide the ability to perform point-in-time-restores for application recovery (with an adequate time window for the various pricing tiers) and Geo-Replication for disaster recovery.

Setting up firewall rules

Azure SQL database has a built-in firewall engine to protect the endpoint from remote IPs. In conjunction with a good user roles policy, and encrypted connection, it offers a good level of security. The SQL Database firewall configuration is available in the **CONFIGURE** tab of the Management Portal for a given SQL Database Server. There are three kinds of rules available:

- Allowing access from any Azure Service
- Allowing access from a specific IP range for the entire server
- Allowing access from a specific IP range for a specific database

The first option is available during the database creation or by flagging the option below:

This rule enables all of Azure's assets to connect to the database, even if outside the region hosting it (for example, a VM running in the US can connect to a database running in Europe, with this rule enabled).

The second option is available in the same tab, specifying which IP ranges are allowed:

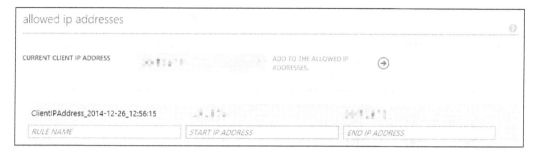

The third option is available using the `sp_set_database_firewall_rule` stored procedure. To execute this, connect to the desired database and execute the following command:

```
exec sp_set_database_firewall_rule N'PermitPackt',
  '83.166.169.231','83.166.169.231'
```

> At the time of writing this book, the previous IP address points to the PacktPub.com website. We can also set up a *permit all* firewall rule with the range, 0.0.0.0 – 255.255.255.255. However, it is not recommended since it completely invalidates the purpose of the firewall.

To verify the firewall configuration, we can use the following SQL views:

- At a server level: `sys.firewall_rules`
- At a database level: `sys.database_firewall_rules`

> In the results pane, a firewall rule named `AllowAllWindowsAzureIps` (or with a **Globally Unique Identifier** (**GUID**)) could be shown, with the starting and ending addresses equal to 0.0.0.0. This rule is added by the Azure Portal when the user chooses to allow the Azure Services to access the database (the Yes/No toggle in the server of the **CONFIGURE** tab).

Setting up users and roles

Except for the administrative credentials (the `sa` - equivalent of SQL Server) we create during the SQL Database Server provisioning, we can create custom users and roles for a given SQL Database instance. The basic rule is:

- A login is required to login to the server
- A user is required to access the database

To create a user with specific permission to a given database, proceed as follows:

1. Open a **New Query** window into the master database, and create a login:

```
CREATE LOGIN myTestLogin WITH PASSWORD=
   'UseAStrongPasswordPleaseee';
```

2. Move to a **New Query** window on the desired database, and create the database user for the login:

```
CREATE USER myTestUser FROM LOGIN myTestLogin;
```

3. Assign db_owner permissions to the newly created database user:

```
EXEC sp_addrolemember 'db_owner', 'myTestUser';
```

4. Connect to **SQL Server Management Studio** (**SSMS**) using the newly created credentials (use myTestLogin as a username), specifying the desired database instead of the default (master) one.

To view the current set of server logins, this query can be executed:

```
select * from sys.sql_logins
```

The minimum permission set to manage server-level security is the loginmanager role (to create logins) and the dbmanager role (to create databases). At the database level security, we can also grant specific permissions, as we would do in the on-premise SQL Server engine.

While implementing multi-tenant solutions, it is common to create boundaries between tenants, isolating their data, to enforce security overall. Assuming we have a single database with each tenant in a separate database schema, we can easily create a role that is bound to that tenant from which users can be created hierarchically:

1. Connect to the desired database, open a **New Query** window and execute this command:

```
CREATE ROLE customRole
```

2. Grant the reading permission on a selected schema to the created role:

```
GRANT SELECT ON SCHEMA :: mySchema TO customRole
```

3. Add an existing user (or create a new one following the preceding step) to the role:

```
EXEC sp_addrolemember N'customRole', N'myTestUser'
```

When connecting to the database with the designated user, you will see only the table owned by the schema specified in step 2.

Connection settings

When a SQL Database Server is provisioned, it is assigned a fully qualified DNS name in the form, `SERVER_NAME.database.windows.net`. A database name must be provided when the SQL Database is created. SQL Database logins are created in precisely the same way they are in Microsoft SQL Server, as we saw earlier. It is conventional to specify SQL Database logins in the form, `LOGIN@SERVER_NAME`, even when it is not required. All communications of the SQL Database are over an encrypted channel and it is recommended that the server certificate used with this channel not be trusted. This leads to a connection string, as shown:

```
Data Source=SERVER_NAME.database.windows.net;

Initial Catalog=DATABASE_NAME;User ID=LOGIN@SERVER_NAME;

Password=PASSWORD;Encrypt=True;TrustServerCertificate=False
```

This connection string can be retrieved from the application configuration or created using the `SqlConnectionStringBuilder` class. Note that SQL Database forces the connection to be encrypted, even if the client does not specify encryption. The `TrustServerCertificate` parameter forces the client to validate the server certificate, helping to avoid man-in-the-middle attacks.

With the management views of the SQL Database engine, we can perform troubleshooting and monitoring regarding what is happening to the database, Azure provides also an auditing service to track various events against the database transparently (data access, schema changes, data changes, security failures, grant/revoke permissions). This is done through a special endpoint, called a *security enabled* connection string that changes from the old one for the name of the server endpoint:

- **From**: `SERVER_NAME.database.windows.net`
- **To**: `SERVER_NAME.database.secure.windows.net`

When the **AUDITING** is **ENABLED**, applications can use this endpoint to log all the relevant events to a given Storage Account. It is possible to specify that all the connections to the database must be made against the secure endpoint, by flagging the following option, in the **AUDITING & SECURITY** tab of the Management Portal:

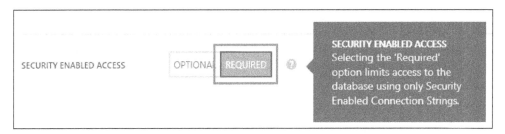

Be aware that users with the appropriate Storage Account Keys of the account where the auditing trace is collected, have access to database-related sensitive data.

Working with a cache

The caching service has been growing faster than in the past due to the growing need for building large-scale web applications. In this section, we talk about the two in-memory caching options supported by Azure: the Azure Managed Cache and the Redis Cache.

Modern software architectures often rely on an in-memory caching system to save frequently accessed data that do not change too often. Some extreme scenarios require us to use the in-memory cache as the primary data store for sensitive data, pursuing design patterns oriented to eventual persistence and consistency.

It is evident that in both cases, the caching service must be protected properly to avoid data loss:

- Cache as copy of frequently accessed data:
    - In case of a malicious deletion, at the first cache miss, the cache generator (the code or some batch procedures) needs to again fetch the current data from the data store, causing a performance delay
    - In case of a malicious modification, the code can behave in unexpected ways, potentially causing huge damage (think about changing the prices of a catalog cache for an online commerce site)

- Cache as primary data store with eventual persistence:
    - In case of a malicious deletion or modification, since the caching system owns the most recent and valid version of the data, the entire system can be compromised

In the following section, we discuss how to enforce security on both Azure Managed Cache and Azure Redis Cache.

Azure Managed Cache

Azure Managed Cache is the evolution of the former AppFabric Cache for the Windows Server and it is a managed in-memory cache service. From the intrinsic security perspective, the standard and premium tiers offer high availability, which means a replication of cached objects for resiliency against hardware failures.

However, from the user's perspective, it adheres to the same security model as a Storage Account. When a Managed Cache instance is created (now only done through PowerShell commands) the access details are identified by:

- **Cache name**: the one chosen during creation
- **Access keys (primary and secondary)**: the keys to be used in applications
- **Cache endpoint**: the URL, in the form `[cacheName].cache.windows.net`, to connect to the service

As in the case of the Storage Account, losing the Access key could result in serious security implications.

SSL

By default, communication between a client and a cache is not encrypted. An unencrypted connection could be used for communication between clients and the cache in the same Azure region, based on the assumption that being in the same region makes the communication already secure. However, if this is not possible we need to ensure all the communication happens over TLS; in C#, we can do this as follows:

```
var configuration = new DataCacheFactoryConfiguration()
{
  AutoDiscoverProperty=new DataCacheAutoDiscoverProperty
    (enable:true,identifier:endpoint),
  IsCompressionEnabled=true,
  MaxConnectionsToServer=2,
  SecurityProperties = new DataCacheSecurity
    (authorizationToken:key,sslEnabled:true),
};
var factory = new DataCacheFactory(configuration);
```

`AutoDiscoverProperty` is set to true, which means we do not need to specify the TCP connection ports for the service (in addition to the endpoint). `MaxConnectionsToServer` is useful to limit (or control) the maximum concurrent connections between the client and the cache service; finally, `SecurityProperties` defines both the Access key and the SSL connection.

This can also be done in `app/web.config`:

```
<dataCacheClients>
  <dataCacheClient name="default">
    <autoDiscover isEnabled="true"
    identifier="[cacheName].cache.windows.net" />
```

```
    <securityProperties mode="Message" sslEnabled="true">
      <messageSecurity authorizationInfo="[authKey]" />
    </securityProperties>
  </dataCacheClient>
</dataCacheClients>
```

Named caches

Every Azure Managed Cache endpoint has a default named cache. A named cache can be represented as a slice of the entire cache, isolated from the others. Despite the total size of the cache, it is shared between the various named caches (and multiple named caches are available only at standard and premium tiers), and this is a good way to split the cache in logically separated domains.

In fact, when it is not possible (due to cost reasons) to create a cache for each service (or for each Dev/Test/Staging environment), named caches can be used to achieve isolation. Finally, since it is not possible to infer or obtain the various names of named caches from within the cache usage (through either the `DataCacheFactory` or `DataCache` objects), a good isolation practice is to give named caches complex names, as follows:

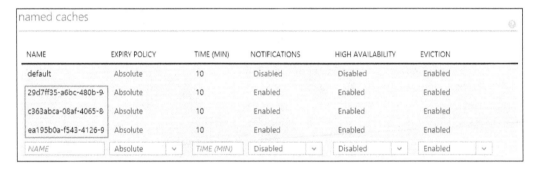

NAME	EXPIRY POLICY	TIME (MIN)	NOTIFICATIONS	HIGH AVAILABILITY	EVICTION
default	Absolute	10	Disabled	Disabled	Enabled
29d7ff35-a6bc-480b-9	Absolute	10	Enabled	Enabled	Enabled
c363abca-08af-4065-8	Absolute	10	Enabled	Enabled	Enabled
ea195b0a-f543-4126-9	Absolute	10	Enabled	Enabled	Enabled
NAME	Absolute ⌄	TIME (MIN)	Disabled ⌄	Disabled ⌄	Enabled ⌄

This can add an additional layer of security in case the Access key is lost.

 Be aware that a malicious user with the valid cache credentials can influence the security of named caches the same way, by over-consuming resources on the default named cache, or by occupying the entire caching space.

For the regeneration and rotation of the keys, the same principles as in the case of Storage Accounts apply.

Azure Redis Cache

Redis is an open source, high performance data store written in ANSI C: as its name stands for Remote Dictionary Server, it is a key value data store with optional durability. Since its wide adoption in 2010, it became one of the most popular in-memory caches and also NoSQL data stores. Redis has been designed (according to this documentation article, refer to `http://redis.io/topics/security`):

> *to be accessed by trusted clients inside trusted environments. [...]*
> *it is not a good idea to expose the Redis instance directly to the*
> *Internet [...] In general, Redis is not optimized for maximum*
> *security but for maximum performance and simplicity.*

In Redis, ACLs are not supported; however, Azure Redis Cache can be configured with two security measures:

- Primary and secondary Access keys
- A secure endpoint

Throughout this chapter, Access keys have been discussed a lot, since they are used to authenticate clients and used to perform rolling updates transparently. A client holding the Redis endpoint name (in the form: `[chosenName].redis.cache.windows.net`) plus one of the Access keys has full rights against the Redis cache.

This is why, by default, the non-secure endpoint is disabled, forcing clients to use the **SSL PORT** (`6380`), as shown here:

If the Redis cache is going to be accessed by internal services only, (inside the same Azure region), the non-secure endpoint can be enabled to reduce the communication overhead.

Databases

Although a user holding the endpoint name and an Access key can perform every kind of action against the Redis instance, a way to isolate a tenant's data can be implemented by using databases. Redis has one default database (the 0 DB) and it supports up to 16 databases with standard configuration. Each database may have its own keys, meaning two different databases on the same instance may save different values with the same key. This method, as the named caches for the Azure Managed Cache, might help while implementing isolation between the tenant's data. However, a generic user can always enumerate DBs and keys, making it just a logical boundary.

Finally, when the Redis website announced the future availability of a Redis Cluster, (refer to http://redis.io/topics/cluster-tutorial) the databases feature became deprecated and its usage is not recommended for new projects anymore. It is reasonable to assume, however, that databases will be discontinued only for Redis Cluster implementations, while the non-cluster modes will continue to use them.

Working with the Service Bus

Azure Service Bus is a Cloud-based messaging solution that provides a robust infrastructure while connecting different endpoints. Although Microsoft releases new features continuously, Azure Service Bus is already a very complete platform, composed by:

- **Queues**: An entity supporting brokered messages where there are one or more *producers* and one or more *consumers*. A queue is often used to decouple systems and to perform asynchronous communication/computation between parties.

- **Topics**: An entity supporting brokered messages where there are one or more *publishers* and one or more *subscribers*. The differences with the queues are many, but the most important is that a published message is propagated to every valid subscriber, making it suitable for notification mechanisms, while queues are more suitable for processing (a message is processed by only one receiver, if multiple).

- **Event Hubs**: A feature specially designed to ingest high volumes of messages, persisting them somewhere for further analytical processing by worker processes.

- **Notification Hubs**: A feature specially designed to send high volumes of push notifications to several devices, with different platform notification systems.

- **Relay Services**: A feature which enables an arbitrary WCF service, residing in some place somewhere (with Internet connectivity), to be exposed to the public Internet through an Azure-managed relay service.

The Service Bus namespace is the top-level subscription item, which contains one or more entities of the types above. To get access to an entity of the namespace, a client should sign the resource request with a valid Access key that belongs to an existing Shared Access Policy.

 In the past, when a user created a new Service Bus namespace, the Azure Portal also created an **Access Control Service** (**ACS**) namespace, linking them to provide a fully featured claims-based authentication solution. However, this solution is not recommended anymore either, because there are no public announcements about the future of ACS, or because for many scenarios, a simpler access architecture based on Shared Access Signatures is, often, good enough.

Shared Access Policies

When a user creates an Azure Services Bus namespace, a default **Shared Access Policy** (**SAP**) gets created in the **CONFIGURE** tab of the Management Portal. A SAP is a definition of access rights, along with a policy name and primary/secondary keys, as follows:

In the preceding figure, two additional SAPs have been added to the namespace:

- **Sender**: This policy has a send-only permission to the assets created in the whole namespace
- **Receiver**: This policy has a receive-only permission to the assets created in the whole subscription

It is very important to avoid the usage of `RootManageSharedAccessKey` (or a user-created equivalent policy), since it has full rights to the whole namespace. A client with these credentials can create/delete entities as well as objects inside these entities. This can impact the confidentiality, integrity, and availability of an entire platform.

Instead, we can create a specific SAP for an entity, ensuring that permissions are given, at the most, to the specific entity without compromising the entire namespace. Each entity can declare a maximum of 12 SAPs.

To create a SAP for a given entity (a specific queue, for example) we can either go to the **CONFIGURE** tab of the entity, or we can use the SDK, as follows:

```
//connStr = "Endpoint=sb://[name].servicebus.windows.net/;
//SharedAccessKeyName=[keyName];SharedAccessKey=[keyValue]";
var nm = NamespaceManager.CreateFromConnectionString(connStr);
var queue = new QueueDescription(path:"myQueue");
queue.Authorization.Add(
  new SharedAccessAuthorizationRule
  (
  keyName:"ListenOnQueue",
  primaryKey:SharedAccessAuthorizationRule.GenerateRandomKey(),
  secondaryKey:SharedAccessAuthorizationRule.GenerateRandomKey(),
  rights:new []{AccessRights.Listen}
  )
);
nm.CreateQueue(queue);
```

Clients should use Shared Access Policies to generate the appropriate signatures to operate against the Service Bus.

Summary

In this chapter, we talked about Azure PaaS from a security perspective. We looked at the most important services such as Cloud Services, Websites, storage, SQL Database, cache and Service Bus. We also discussed the security aspects of each service and the best security practices that should be used to protect these services.

In the following chapter, we will discuss IaaS and what we need to know from a security perspective.

Infrastructure as a Service

Customers choosing IaaS usually have existing project constraints, which are not adaptive to PaaS. We can think about a complex installation of an enterprise-level software suite, like an ERP or a SharePoint farm. This is one of the cases where a service like an Azure website probably cannot fit.

As mentioned in the previous chapter, PaaS is probably the future of Cloud computing and we should expect investments in PaaS to overcome the existing limits which lead clients to an IaaS product. This said, IaaS is a set of services/products where the customer deals with middle level management. For VMs, for example, this means that everything is happening on the operating system.

To remind you of which things you need to manage in different scenarios, take a look at this image:

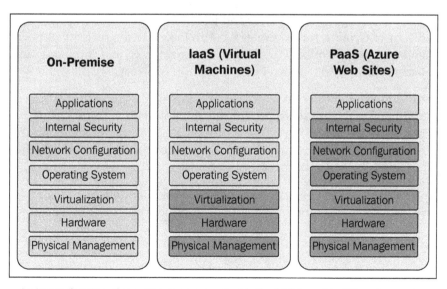

An image showing what customers manage (inside the thick boxes) in different scenarios.

This image shows that with an **On-Premise** infrastructure, we need to directly manage everything, including the physical layer. With **IaaS** (VMs, for instance) we need to manage things apart from the physical layer. Finally, for the big picture, using **PaaS** we only have to think about the actual applications to run.

Microsoft Azure provides the security infrastructure to safely connect different services but, with IaaS, we often need to implement measures by ourselves (or, at least, be aware of the threats).

There are two main services where the security requirements should be correctly understood and addressed:

- Azure Virtual Machines
- Azure Virtual Networks

Regarding the first service, VMs, we delve into what could be considered external security, namely, every measure to be taken on a VM, with regard to the outside aspects. Thinking of a VM as a black box, we instead define internal security as the various aspects (related to security) implemented in the VM. The main differences between the two are:

- **External security**: Azure helps to set it up and it is possible to manage it directly from the Azure Portal or PowerShell
- **Internal security**: It is up to the customer, defined and managed internally, at the operating system level, and is not manageable by Azure

Regarding the second service, **Virtual Networks** (**VNets**), we see how these are important to achieve good security and isolation patterns, by implementing Network Security Groups, for example. We also look into the security opportunities while interconnecting premises, building hybrid networks, and implementing advanced scenarios.

Azure also provides some services for cross-premises disaster recovery: site recovery (not covered here) is the option to provide a company with various VM replication patterns, while Azure Backup provides a durable and enterprise-level backup solution for both the Windows Server and the Windows Client remote machines (either in a Cloud Service or on-premise).

This chapter shows you the most important Azure IaaS building blocks and highlights the security aspects of VMs and VNets, and also introduces the Azure Backup service.

Virtual Machines

VMs are the most configurable execution environments for applications that Azure provides. With VMs, we can run arbitrary workloads, custom tools, and applications, but we need to manage and maintain them directly, including the security.

Physical security is, however, handled by Microsoft, as well as every measure to guarantee the logical isolation between different customers.

External security

As mentioned before, external security refers to all those measures that we can provide exclusive of the running VM. Taking VM as a black box model, external security involves what happens outside it.

Before having control over a VM, we need to first create it. Regarding the underlying operating system, a different setup could be required for Linux and Windows, for example. After doing this, in a basic scenario, we would probably want to connect to that instance to administrate it. In order to do this, we configure the endpoints and ACLs.

How does isolation help in building safe solutions? Moreover, how does Azure isolate VMs of the same customer/subscription, but of a different tenant/environment?

In this section, we are going to inspect these aspects:

- VM creation
- Endpoints and ACLs
- Networking and isolation
- Microsoft Antimalware

Creation: Windows versus Linux

VMs can be created by using the current Azure Management Portal, the Preview portal, via PowerShell, or through the Management API (and its related clients). In the following pictures and documentation, we use the current portal. Despite the Preview portal, there are many new configurable options during the VM setup:

- Time zone and updates
- Domain Join
- VNets and IP addresses
- Resource groups and diagnostics

While creating a new Windows VM, a few (but important) security settings are needed:

- **Administrator username**: The portal always blocks usernames containing common words, such as admin or administrator.

- **Administrator password**: The portal asks for a secure password (a minimum of eight characters, with at least three lowercase/uppercase/number/special characters).

- **Storage Account**: The portal suggests that you create an independent Storage Account to hold the **Virtual Hard Disk (VHD)** images of the operating system. This is important because someone accessing a Storage Account, shared between VMs and custom applications, can easily download or even change the contents of a VHD.

> It is a good practice to create a specific Storage Account for VM's VHDs. However, since the creation of a new Storage Account for each VM can be expensive (in terms of management), a good practice is to hold all the VHDs in a specific (but single) Storage Account, giving administrators the least access privileges.

- **Endpoints**: The portal suggests two default endpoints pointing to the new VM - **Remote Desktop** and **PowerShell**. In the **ENDPOINTS** section, we will see how this involves security:

ENDPOINTS			
NAME	PROTOCOL	PUBLIC PORT	PRIVATE PORT
Remote Desktop	TCP	AUTO	3389
PowerShell	TCP	5986	5986
ENTER OR SELECT A VALUE ⌄			

- **VM Agent**: The portal suggests installing the VM Agent by default in the newly created instance. This is an important security aspect, since the VM Agent is actually an entry point to the VM operating system, in addition to the Remote Desktop and PowerShell ones. This also means that, in case of losing the administrative credentials, VM Agent is the only actor which will be able to inject new credentials in a given instance.

While creating a new Linux VM, instead, these settings are required:

- **Administrator username**: The portal behaves similar to the one on Windows.

- **Administrator password**: The portal behaves similar to the one on Windows.

- **Administrator SSH Key**: The portal lets us also create the administrator profile by entering an SSH Key (usually in a .pem file generated with tools like OpenSSL). This is generally more secure than a simple password, but human beings cannot memorize it. An article explaining how to generate SSH keys can be found at `http://azure.microsoft.com/en-us/documentation/articles/virtual-machines-linux-use-ssh-key/`.

- **Storage Account**: The portal behaves similar to the one on Windows.

- **Endpoints**: The portal suggests a single default endpoint to connect to the VM. Since there is no PowerShell or Remote Desktop on Linux, the SSH endpoint is the only entry point to manage the actual instance.

- **VM Agent**: The portal installs the VM Agent by default, and it cannot be disabled, except from inside the instance. A complete guide to the Azure Linux Agent can be found at `http://azure.microsoft.com/en-us/documentation/articles/virtual-machines-linux-agent-user-guide/`.

Microsoft Open Technologies created an interesting community repository project named **VM Depot**, which let users choose an operating system image (along with a preinstalled software and configuration) from a variety of public Linux and FreeBSD VM images. It is possible to import an existing image in an active subscription, and use it while building new VMs, either from the Azure Portal or the VM Depot website (refer to `https://vmdepot.msopentech.com/List/Index`):

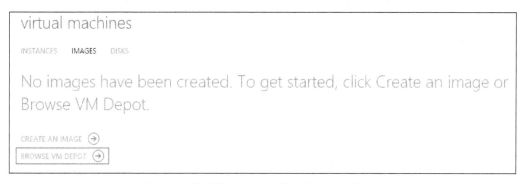

Browsing VM Depot from within the Azure Portal

From a security perspective, this is obviously other users' code and configuration, so we need to be aware of this while setting up real-world workloads or exposing sensitive data.

Endpoints and ACLs

Superseding an Azure Virtual Machine, there is always a Cloud Service, which is a sort of container of VMs, with a public IP address, which is exposed to the Internet. Each VM created under the same Cloud Service name, also known as **Deployment** (if the user created a service named `myService`, then the URL would be `myService.cloudapp.net`) will be accessible through this name and specific port, if not specified otherwise.

To explain the concept better, see the following image:

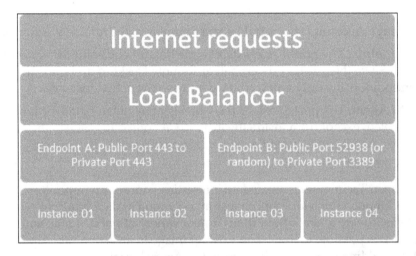

In the preceding image, a **Load Balancer** stands between the Internet and the VMs (called Instance XX). The **Load Balancer**, which is actually represented by the Cloud Service name, defines some endpoints (such as **Endpoint A** and **Endpoint B** in the picture); each endpoint maps a public port to a private port along with the protocol type (TCP or UDP).

Endpoints defined in the **ENDPOINTS** tab of a given VM are related to a single VM only. It means that we cannot configure, for example, the same TCP Port 80 for two VMs in the same Cloud Service, except in the case where we declare a load-balanced set (not covered in this book).

During the creation of a VM, the portal suggests that you include two default endpoints for the Windows OS (RDP and PowerShell), as long as one default endpoint is for the Linux OS (SSH). It is a good practice to remap the public port of an endpoint to a random one, so as to limit the number of potential attacks on well-known ports.

An endpoint comes with a default permit-all IP-based ACL. This behavior can be overridden by defining the custom ACLs, as follows:

The basic rules are:

- Specify up to 50 ACL rules per VM endpoint
- Use IPv4 **Classless Inter-Domain Routing (CIDR)** addresses to permit/deny traffic
- Use combinations and orders of rules to implement advanced scenarios

Considering the Remote Desktop endpoint, a good security practice could be to block everything except the remote subnet (or IP address) used to connect to the VM:

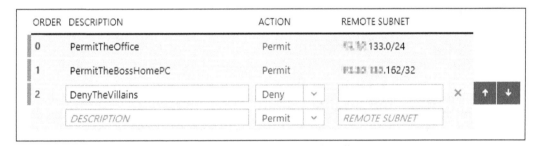

In the preceding screenshot, we setup ACLs to permit traffic from an IP range (rule zero), then allow a single IP (rule one), and finally block a hypothetical IP range. However, in case of permit rules, everything except the addresses permitted are blocked by default: rule two is, therefore, useless.

Using ACLs to limit inbound traffic to a VM is a good enough measure to protect an endpoint. Another measure is to move the responsibility of the blocking logic inside the VM, by setting up a firewall rule, as we will see in the *Internal security* section later in this chapter.

Networking and isolation

By default, every VM created on the portal ships with only the remote management endpoints enabled; this means that all other Internet traffic is blocked by default. With endpoints and ACLs, we can configure which ports can be accessed from the Internet. For a more refined control, we can even filter the exact IP range(s) allowed to use the endpoints.

We can see that a Cloud Service can also be called a Deployment, since it groups several different VMs in a single logical container. This container, as for the PaaS, permits communication between the VMs inside it through private IP addresses. Therefore, by default, VMs in different deployments cannot communicate with each other, except when they are deployed to a common Virtual Network, as shown here:

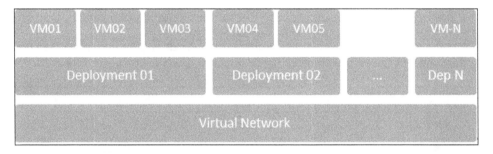

While deploying an application requiring a cross-deployment communication that cannot flow through a private VNet, remember that the Public VIP of the deployment has probably been used. In this case, all the communication can transit over Internet publically, as well as in cases of cross-region communication.

An example of cross-region communication is when a web tier located in Europe accesses a database tier in the US, or vice-versa, cross-region traffic transits over a WAN and is more exposed to security threats.

Azure implements a DDoS defense system from outside and inside attackers (other tenants). As mentioned in *Microsoft Azure Security Whitepaper* (refer to http://download.microsoft.com/download/C/A/3/CA3FC5C0-ECE0-4F87-BF4B-D74064A00846/AzureNetworkSecurity_v2_Oct2014.pdf):

> *Network-layer high volume attacks choke network pipes and packet processing capabilities. The Azure DDoS defense technology provides detection and mitigation techniques such as SYN cookies, rate limiting, and connection limits to help ensure that such attacks do not impact customer environments.*

However, it is also specified:

> *Application-layer attacks can be launched against a customer VM. Azure does not provide mitigation or actively block network traffic affecting individual customer deployments, because the infrastructure does not interpret the expected behavior of customer applications.*

In such a case, a good web application firewall or an application proxy can be placed between the Internet and the VMs, to provide an additional layer of security.

Service Gateway is an open source application proxy, providing protection (authentication/authorization and, in future, DoS/DDoS protection), monitoring (web logs collection and process and analytics), and lifecycle management (A/B testing and custom routing) to an Internet facing web application. A typical scenario in an application proxy is this:

- Client requests are given to a given domain point in the Service Gateway
- The Service Gateway performs its actions and forwards the traffic to the actual Azure asset

The asset involved by the SG can be hosted on IaaS or PaaS.

The SG can be deployed in a Cloud Service. The service package and configuration is available at `https://sg.codeplex.com`. There is also a Service Gateway Management web application, which can be installed on Azure Websites, and it is also available in the Website Gallery (it requires minimal configuration):

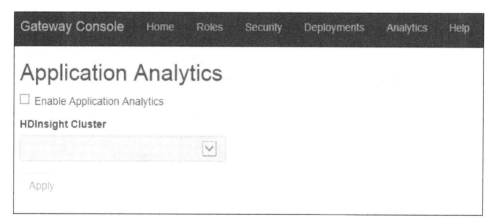

The "Analytics" tab of the Service Gateway Management Console web application.

Extensions

Extensions are pluggable modules which can be installed in a VM as an administrative, declarative task. Two of the most relevant extensions of security in VMs are the Microsoft Antimalware and the Azure Diagnostics.

The Antimalware module is an Azure extension available to both Cloud Services and VMs. For a complete overview of it, read *Chapter 3*, *Platform as a Service* where we investigated the Microsoft Antimalware service in Cloud Services.

For VMs, however, the service is configurable through the Azure Portal and Visual Studio (in addition to other methods, that is, PowerShell, as discussed before). The Antimalware module is also known as an extension, since Azure can plug into several modules of VMs as they are just extensions of the operating instance.

 The Antimalware extension is available for Windows VMs only. The extension is free but it can generate costs due to the data generated and stored as a result of the monitoring operations.

For instances provisioned in the second half of 2014, the VM Agent, along with the Microsoft Antimalware and the BGInfo extensions are probably already installed in the VM. However, to add the extensions (or overwrite the existing configuration, if already installed), we need to:

1. Locate the VM to work on in the Preview portal.

 In order to successfully install extensions, the source image of the VM must be a platform image. This process does not work in user images.

2. Open the **Extensions** blade and select the **Antimalware** extension:

3. Configure the options:

    ○ Excluded files and locations (that is, trusted locations)

    ○ Excluded file extensions (that is, custom scripts, in case of a development machine)

    ○ Excluded processes (that is, the executable names of custom trusted processes)

    ○ Real-time protection and scheduled scans

The Antimalware extension can write logs to a custom Storage Account, using the **Microsoft Monitoring Agent Diagnostics** extension. This can be installed from within Visual Studio, as follows:

- Locate the VM in the Azure => **Virtual Machine** node of the Server Explorer

- Right-click on it and configure it; a list of **Installed Extensions** will show up:

Installed Extensions			
Name	Publisher	Version	Enabled
Windows Azure BGinfo Extension for IaaS	Microsoft.Compute	1.*	☑
Microsoft Antimalware	Microsoft.Azure.Security	1.*	☑

Microsoft Monitoring Agent Diagnostics | Add | Remove | Configure...

- Add the desired extension (**Microsoft Monitoring Agent Diagnostics**); a configuration popup window will appear

- Enter the Storage Account credentials; confirm and save the configuration

Alternatively, to enable a Diagnostics event collection for a VM, enter any of the monitoring parts in the VM blade, click on the **Diagnostics** button on the top menu, select **ON** in the **Diagnostics** status and provide a valid storage account and the desired logs to be collected. It will automatically install the Diagnostics extension.

Internal security

This section does not even try to cover Windows security, since the topic requires a full length book on its own. However, there are a few best practices for developers and beginners, which can help to achieve a good level of internal security. Since we defined external security as the group of measures we can implement outside the operating system area (and consequently outside the VM security boundary), internal security is used to define the set of measures required to secure the OS and user applications.

To summarize the basic concepts of internal security, we are going to cover:

- Operating system firewalls
- Auditing and best practices

Operating system firewall

We can implement ACLs on the various VM endpoints to provide an external firewall to the VM. Alternatively, to gain more control over the ports/IPs/services to allow/deny, we can use the Windows Firewall with Advanced Security. Quoting the Microsoft Technet documentation (refer to `https://technet.microsoft.com/en-us/library/dd759063.aspx`):

> *Windows Firewall with Advanced Security is a stateful firewall that inspects and filters all packets for IP version 4 (IPv4) and IP version 6 (IPv6) traffic. In this context, filter means to allow or block network traffic by processing it through administrator-defined rules. By default, incoming traffic is blocked unless it is a response to a request by the host (solicited traffic) or it is specifically allowed (that is, a firewall rule has been created to allow the traffic). You can configure Windows Firewall with Advanced Security to explicitly allow traffic by specifying a port number, application name, service name, or other criteria.*

A scenario where the OS firewall may help is, for example, when we want to block outbound traffic. In certain cases, a server should not open any HTTP connections to the outside world. For this, a firewall rule must be configured, as follows:

1. Open the **Windows Firewall with Advanced Security** (later referred to as *Firewall*).
2. Locate the **Outbound Rules** section and create a **New Rule...**.
3. Select **Custom** as the rule type.
4. Select **All programs** as the program.
5. In the **Protocol and Ports** section:
   - Select **TCP** and in the **Remote port**, select **Specific Ports**
   - Enter 80, 443 into the specific ports
6. Leave the default scopes (any IP address) in the **Scope** window.
7. Select **Block the connection** as the **Action**.
8. Select all the three Profiles (**Domain, Private, Public**) and give the rule a name.

Firewall can also help in isolating VMs within the same Virtual Network. As we will see in the *Virtual Networks* section later in the chapter, a VM can be deployed into a VNet, which has a private IP accessible only from within the VNet itself.

Auditing and best practices

Microsoft, with Azure, implemented a robust and secure environment to run services, but, since there are many configuration options for us to choose from, assets can be exploited in several ways. It is quite unimportant to say this, but we need to focus on:

- **Strong passwords**: Brute force attacks still exist and we need to be aware of them. In addition to the password complexity requirements, I would say there should be a *password policy* in place, providing rules about the complexity, changing frequency, forbidden words, lockout, and so on.

- **Detect brute force attacks**: By auditing failed logins, an administrator can detect an attempt to attack before a malicious user takes control of the machine.

 In case of remotely managed VMs like in Azure, the RDP endpoint is very often opened to the Internet, publically. "Okay," we say, "We have remapped the remote RDP port to a random one," but, of course, this is just an entry-level measure. Anti-intrusion software can detect multiple login attempts, providing out-of-the-box actions to reduce the risks (by dynamically blocking the remote IPs that are performing the attack).

- **Avoid installing unnecessary software**: Unnecessary software increments the security risks by adding useless complexity to the operating system. In addition to this, untrusted software or software from unverified sources can be potentially dangerous. Apply this purposeful question to these kind of situations - *Would you let a promising but unknown person put his or her stuff in your house?*

- **Do not shortcut procedures**: It is quite common to bypass standard processes in case of an exception, especially when some critical event takes place. The administrators of VM should not perform quick fixes to VM that are not quick fixes at all; they are often, instead, potential generators of new security issues.

Finally, a good auditing policy must be set in place to check against various events occurring on the VM. The Windows Server has a great built-in support to audit entire operating systems. Basic auditing on Logon events, however, are enabled by default. To get an idea of auditing, we can:

1. Open the **Event Viewer** and select the **Windows Logs | Security** logs.

2. Filter the results providing the ID, **4625** (an account failed to log on).

3. If some records appear, inspect the logs to find out the reason for the failures.

An example of a failed logon attempt is as follows:

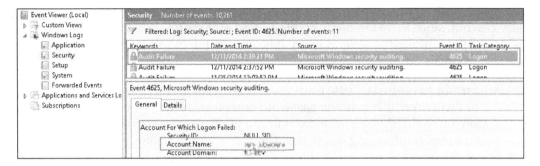

There are many books about Windows Server security, as well as Linux security, we do not cover everything in this section. These simple notes are just pointers to keep in mind.

Virtual Networks

The first thing to ask about VNets is: do we need a VNet? VNet is a service used to build a private network into the Azure Cloud to perform the following:

- **Extend the security boundary of Cloud Services and VMs**: several Cloud Services and VMs can be placed in a single VNet to let them communicate without passing from the Internet publically

- **Set up a Hybrid solution**: If we need to connect an existing on-premise infrastructure to Azure, VNet is the starting point

These two reasons (though they are not the only ones) are consistent with the two modes of how VNet can be deployed:

- **Cloud-only VNet**: This is the choice to enable the first scenario

- **Cross-premises VNet**: This is the choice that offers much more flexibility

From the security perspective, there are two connected, main security points (in addition to what we have already covered before):

- **Cross-service communication**: Several VMs in different Cloud Services can communicate with each other if they are in the same VNet. This is a benefit but also an extension to the isolation boundary.

- **Public endpoints exposure**: Similar to the previous point, a VM which is not properly configured, with a public endpoint to the Internet, can be the entry point for an attack to other VMs (though they are apparently in a safe place) on the VNet:

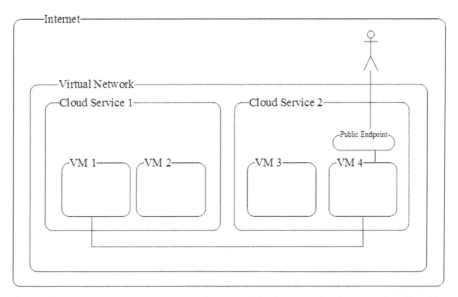

This figure shows that a user can get access to the VM 1 (which is securely placed inside a Cloud Service without public endpoints) through a public endpoint of the VM 4 (that is placed under another Cloud Service, but due to the VNet communication, it is able to reach VM 1).

Network Security Groups

Network Security Groups (NSG) help to implement some secure scenarios, including the ones discussed in the previous section. As we can already define an ACL for a public endpoint of a VM, we had discussed that anyone could get access to a private network through a bounce in the public endpoint. NSGs are an advanced set of rules applicable to single VMs or entire subnets.

With NSGs, we can demonstrate this scenario, as follows:

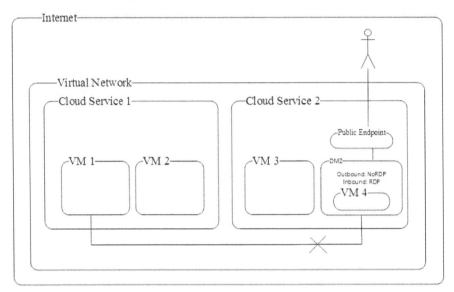

In this version, VM4 outbound RDP connections are restricted due to a "DMZ" Network Security Group, while the inbound RDP connection is still allowed.

NSGs are a transparent layer of security, which can be attached to a single VM or to entire subnets. The NSG configuration is available only through PowerShell (or the API); the configuration shown in the preceding image can be implemented as follows:

1. Open Microsoft Azure PowerShell (the minimum version you must have is 0.8.10).

2. If you haven't already linked to the Azure account, use the `Add-AzureAccount` command.

3. Select the desired subscription with the `Select-AzureSubscription` command.

4. Create the NSG as follows:

   ```
   New-AzureNetworkSecurityGroup -Name "DMZ" -Location "West
       Europe" -Label "DMZ"
   ```

5. Create the outbound rule as follows:

   ```
   Get-AzureNetworkSecurityGroup -Name "DMZ" | Set-
       AzureNetworkSecurityRule -Name "NoRDP" -Type Outbound -
       Priority 100 -Action Deny -SourceAddressPrefix * -
       SourcePortRange * -DestinationAddressPrefix * -
       DestinationPortRange 3389 -Protocol TCP
   ```

6. Create the inbound rule as follows:

```
Get-AzureNetworkSecurityGroup -Name "DMZ" | Set-
  AzureNetworkSecurityRule -Name "RDP" -Type Inbound -
  Priority 200 -Action Allow -SourceAddressPrefix
  "INTERNET" -SourcePortRange * -DestinationAddressPrefix *
  -DestinationPortRange 3389 -Protocol TCP
```

7. Apply the "DMZ" NSG to the specific VM:

```
Get-AzureVM -ServiceName "Cloud-Service-2" -Name "VM-4" |
  Set-AzureNetworkSecurityGroupConfig -
  NetworkSecurityGroupName "DMZ" | Update-AzureVM
```

During the process, this screen appears, showing the DMZ group with its rules:

```
DMZ

   Type: Inbound

Name              Priority  Action   Source Address   Source Port  Destination      Destination   Protocol
                                     Prefix           Range        Address Prefix   Port Range
RDP               200       Allow    INTERNET         *            *                3389          TCP
ALLOW UNET INBOUND 65000    Allow    VIRTUAL_NETWORK  *            VIRTUAL_NETWORK  *             *
ALLOW AZURE LOAD  65001     Allow    AZURE_LOADBALAN  *            *                *             *
BALANCER INBOUND                     CER
DENY ALL INBOUND  65500     Deny     *                *            *                *             *

   Type: Outbound

Name              Priority  Action   Source Address   Source Port  Destination      Destination   Protocol
                                     Prefix           Range        Address Prefix   Port Range
NoRDP             100       Deny     *                *            *                3389          TCP
ALLOW UNET OUTBOUND 65000  Allow    VIRTUAL_NETWORK  *            VIRTUAL_NETWORK  *             *
ALLOW INTERNET    65001     Allow    *                *            INTERNET         *             *
OUTBOUND
DENY ALL OUTBOUND 65500     Deny     *                *            *                *             *
```

Now, whoever accesses the **VM 4** via RDP will not be able to initiate any RDP connection to any destination.

Hybrid networks

In Azure, we can create three types of hybrid, cross-premises connections:

- **Site-to-site**: The on-premise branch is connected to the VNet through a VPN device (or the Windows Server 2012 RRAS). Each client in the on-premise network will be connected to the Cloud VNet too.

- **Point-to-site**: A VPN connection is made for each client who connects to the remote VNet.

- **ExpressRoute**: With a specific agreement between a company and a given (and supported) connectivity provider (ISP), the company gets a dedicated connection from its facility to the Azure datacenter. Note that ExpressRoute only supports some ISPs as well as certain Azure regions.

Site-to-site and ExpressRoute are the most secure options we have to enable cross-premises connectivity. Point-to-site, however, exposes the company to potential security issues due to the distributed nature of the solution:

- A remote VPN client can run everywhere
- The certificate can be stolen, copied, or moved

Therefore, point-to-site introduces new risks, which have to be managed with a strong certificate policy (generation, maintenance, and revocation of it).

Azure Backup

Azure Backup helps protect servers or clients against data losses, providing a second place backup solution. In fact, while performing a backup, one of the primary requirements is the location of the backup. Avoid backing up sensitive or critical data to a physical location that is strictly connected to the primary source of the data itself. In case of a disaster involving the facility where the source is located, there is a higher probability that loss of data (including the backup) can occur.

While this is probably the most important aspect of a backup solution, Azure Backup also provides the capability to encrypt backup sets at the source before the data leaves the source machine, with an encryption key that is defined by us.

As it is an enterprise-level service, usable even in very complex scenarios, it integrates with existing backup tools of the Windows Server and the **System Center Data Protection Manager**. It can be configured to minimize the bandwidth consumption, and it provides incremental backups, and point-in-time restoration.

In this last section of the chapter, we see:

- How to configure the backup vault
- How to configure a connected server
- Which backup options we have

Configuring a backup vault

After creating a backup vault in your nearest Azure region (latency, speed, and distance are very important while evaluating a Cloud back up solution), we can use a valid SSL certificate issued by a CA that is trusted by Microsoft, or we can create a valid x.509 v3 certificate with:

- A key length of 2048 (at the very minimum)
- A valid client authentication **Extended Key Usage (EKU)**
- No more than three years of validity

To create a self-signed certificate with these requirements, open an elevated Developer Command Prompt (or just a Command Prompt with the `makecert.exe` command) and execute the following:

```
makecert.exe -r -pe -n CN=CertName -ss my -sr localmachine -eku
    1.3.6.1.5.5.7.3.2 -len 2048 -e 01/01/2018 CertName.cer
```

A `CertName.cer` file will be placed in the folder executing the command, while the complete certificate (along with its private key) is in the personal certificates store.

 The complete certificate should be exported as a PFX file and installed where the Azure Backup Agent runs, so keep it in a safe place.

On the Azure Portal, upload the public part of the certificate, as follows:

The Backup Vault is now configured and ready to register new servers.

Registering a server

After installing it, the Azure Backup Agent (the updated download link is provided in the Azure Portal) has to be connected to the backup vault, by using vault credentials, which are available on the portal as well.

Since the data has been encrypted before it leaves the server, we need to decide and set the encryption passphrase during the server registration process, as follows:

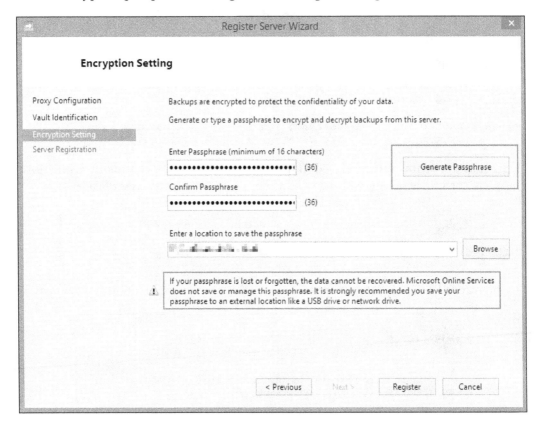

Scheduling backups

After the first configuration, the Microsoft Azure Backup software is very simple and straightforward. We can configure a scheduled backup by following these steps:

1. Click on the **Schedule Backup** action.

2. Add the items to include in the backup.

3. Specify the backup time and retention.

After creating the schedule, the server will automatically synchronize backups to the remote vault.

An important aspect to understand is the retention period. Azure Backup supports up to 120 recovery points, since the recovery mode offers a point-in-time restore service. This means that, in a given time frame, a maximum of 120 points in the past are tracked and recoverable, recycling the older ones one-by-one when the limit is reached.

Consider the following scenario:

- The backup runs each day at 13:00, starting January 1
- After 120 days, we want to recover the status of the oldest version of the data:
  - ° We can recover the initial status of January 1
- The day after (121 days from the beginning), the first available set to recover from is January 2

These assumptions are valid if the backup is completed successfully every day.

Therefore, we can module the schedule to tune the retention period up to 3360 days, according to the following table:

Available recovery points	120			
	Every day	Once a week	Every 2 weeks	Every 4 weeks
Backups in a week	7	1	0,5	0,25
Retention in days	120	840	1680	3360
Retention in years	0,33	2,30	4,60	9,21

The more the retention is, the longer the time between recovery points will be. In case of a maximum retention of 9 years (approximately), the recovery points are four weeks apart from each other.

To get more information on the Azure Backup restoration process, read https://technet.microsoft.com/en-us/library/hh831344.aspx.

Summary

In this chapter, we talked about Azure IaaS from a security perspective. We looked at the most important services, such as VMs and VNets, giving you a quick glance into what is relevant to know while dealing with security aspects. We also investigated the Azure Backup service, which can also be considered as a SaaS service.

In the next chapter, using the same approach, we will inspect some SaaS services.

5

Identity and Access Management for Developers

In *Chapter 2, Identity and Access Management for Users*, we understand the basics of the IAM options for Azure users. This is very important, since our work to implement a fine grained security in each Azure Service can be easily frustrated by a weak administrative authentication mechanism. This is why we talked about the various security options of a Microsoft account, along with the use of Azure AD users to authenticate against Azure itself.

However, Azure AD is a growing IAM service itself with great integration options for custom applications. In *Chapter 3, Platform as a Service* and *Chapter 4, Infrastructure as a Service* we talked about security while using PaaS and IaaS services, respectively. This chapter covers the following:

- Azure AD and ACS
- Azure Key Vault

These two services help developers to build the security aspects of an application. The first, from the developers' perspective, is an IAM service, useful to plug an authentication/authorization logic into a new or existing web application. The second is a new (and still in trial) service, which helps companies to securely store cryptographic keys and application secrets (at the time of writing this book).

> We know that ACS is going to be somehow integrated into Azure AD, according to this blog post written a couple of years ago, http://blogs.technet.com/b/ad/archive/2013/06/22/ azure-active-directory-is-the-future-of-acs.aspx. However, we cover ACS in conjunction with Azure AD to explain its role in the big picture of IAM.

Azure Active Directory

Let's start by telling you what Azure AD isn't. It is not the managed version of the Windows Server AD. Despite its resemblance of the name, Azure AD is *just* an IAM service, managed and hosted by Microsoft in Azure. We should not even try to make a comparison between the two, because they have different scopes and features. It is true that we can link Azure AD with an on-premise AD, but only for the purpose of extending the on-premise AD functionalities to work with Internet-based applications. Throughout this chapter, we look into Azure AD as a stand-alone service without any kind of integration with on-premise environments.

To focus on what the role of Azure AD exactly is, look at this image:

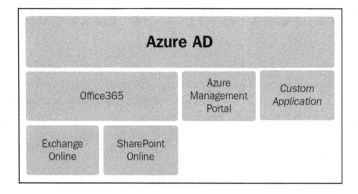

As you can see, different applications can use **Azure AD** as their IAM solution, to provide authentication/authorization for web applications and services. Since **Office 365** or Azure itself uses it to authenticate users, a **Custom Application** can do the same too.

We should assume that we have sufficient knowledge about claims-based authentication to continue reading this chapter; however, let's explain some basics about this:

- **Identity**: It is a set of properties that identifies a user along with its attributes, if any

- **Claim**: It is a piece of identity information, like the e-mail address of a user or the role within an organization

With a claims-based authentication, a simple workflow occurs when:

- The user asks for the resources located at a certain URL
- The application located at this URL checks if, in the HTTP request, there is a valid token issued by someone who's considered to be trusted
    - If not, it redirects the user to the **Identity Provider**, which can be another website, but is trusted by the application
    - The Identity Provider now validates the user credentials (prompting a web page, for example)
    - In case of a successful authentication, the Identity Provider issues a document called security token, where it provides:

        The user information

        An arbitrary number of claims with the properties of the user

    - Before redirecting to the application, the provider signs the token with its private key, so as to certify the validity of the information

- The application receives a security token; it checks if the signature is valid (with the public key of the issuing authority)

 When is a token considered to be valid? The application receiving a token must verify if it is in the expected format, hasn't expired yet, and hasn't been tampered with someone in the middle (or even generated by someone else).
Steps one and two are about parsing, while step three is about verification with the proper key to see whether the signature that came along with the token is valid.

- If a valid security token is found, the application reads who the user is by making the request about its properties

With this technique, there is no need to implement an Identity logic in the application, since it is totally demanded by a third-party, which we call the Identity Provider. This is shown as follows:

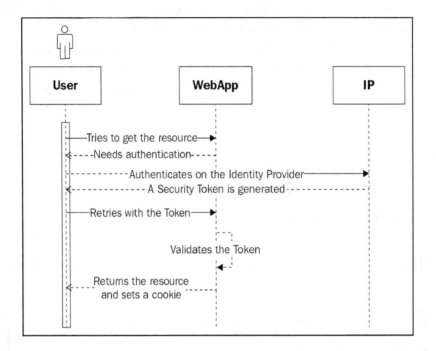

The free eBook, *A Guide to Claims-Based Identity and Access Control* (2nd Edition), *Microsoft patterns & practices* by Vittorio Bertocci, Keith Brown, Scott Densmore, Eugenio Pace, Matias Woloski, and Dominick Baier, is a good way to start learning about the usage of claims-based architectures. The web-based content is also available at https://msdn.microsoft. com/en-us/library/ff423674.aspx.

Think about a basic scenario where we develop a custom web application thinking about every aspect, except the identity. We would like to completely outsource the authentication process along with a whole set of related subprocesses, such as the registration of a new user, the password recovery workflow, and the possibility of a strong authentication mechanism (that is, multifactors). If this is an aspect, we are supposed to plug it without touching the code: this is why claims-based security is a good choice while implementing an authentication strategy for web applications.

Azure AD offers a variety of protocols and message formats to enable a wide range of authentication scenarios; for a complete introduction to these scenarios, read the `https://msdn.microsoft.com/en-us/library/azure/dn499820.aspx`.

As for what we are concerned with, we previously said that Azure AD is organized in tenants (in the form of `tenant.onmicrosoft.com`). A web application can be:

- **Single-tenant**: In this case, the authentication is performed against a single directory (usually one that the organization is developing). Only the tenant's user can successfully log in to the application.

- **Multi-tenant**: In this case, the authentication is performed against multiple directories of different clients. It is to be understood that *external* directories (the ones willing to authenticate themselves into the third-party applications) should be somehow approved and linked.

The integration of an application within Azure AD can be outlined as follows:

1. Obtain the actual URL, where the web application runs (also *localhost-based*, if it is in development stage).

2. Register a new Azure AD application in the Azure Portal. This time, the application is the virtual asset we need to create on Azure, not the real web application itself.

3. Update the web application to use Azure AD as the Identity Provider.

In the following sections, we highlight the principal steps to configure the two scenarios: single-tenant and multi-tenant applications.

Single-tenant applications

The three theoretical steps previously highlighted are technology-independent. Nevertheless, in the following samples, we use ASP.NET as the technology for the web applications and we use Visual Studio 2013 as the development environment.

If we own the appropriate permissions for the Azure subscription and we start from scratch, a Visual Studio template helps to set up both the Azure AD application and the web application configuration, as follows:

1. Create a new ASP.NET project; specify an authentication method:

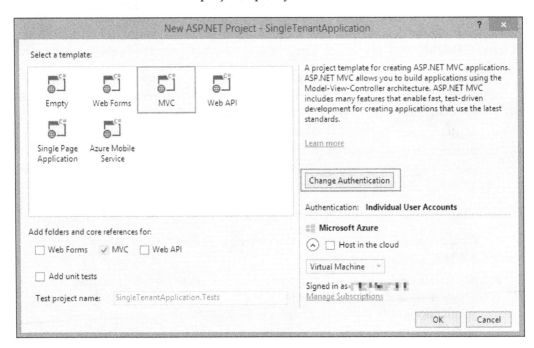

2. Choose **Cloud - Single Organization**, a valid Azure AD directory, and a unique URI for the application (it is just an identifier):

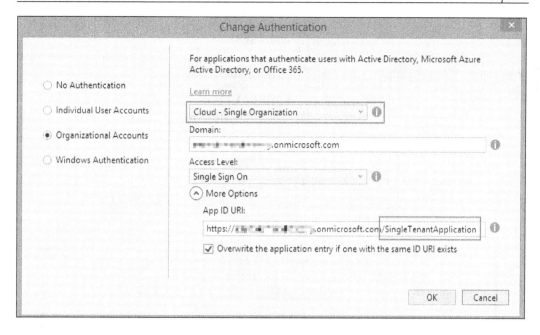

Visual Studio creates a new project with these customized points:

- The `IdentityConfig.cs` class: It is responsible for reading the Federation Metadata endpoint, and obtaining the keys (to validate tokens)

- The `DatabaseIssuerNameRegistry.cs` class: It is responsible for caching the tenants and keys in a local database (it can be changed to meet different scenarios)

- `Web.config`:
    - Settings are added to bind the application with the previously specified unique URI and to import the Federation Metadata XML
    - Handlers and modules are added to handle the incoming security token during the HTTP request, parse it, validate it, and inject its information in the current user session.
    - The login URL for the **Single Sign-On (SSO)** is in the form, `https://login.windows.net/{tenant}.onmicrosoft.com/wsfed`

On the Azure side, Visual Studio also creates an Azure AD application, through the Remote Management APIs (this is why a credential popup is asked for during the creation of a new project). In case we do not want to rely on Visual Studio to create the Azure AD application, we can do this manually, as follows:

1. Go to the current portal, to the **APPLICATIONS** tab of the chosen Azure AD directory and click on **ADD** (in the bottom menu).

2. Select **Add an application my organization is developing**.

3. Give it a name and select **WEB APPLICATION AND/OR WEB API** as the application type.

4. Specify the **SIGN-ON URL** (you can edit this later when the URL is known) and the **App ID URI**.

> While choosing the **App ID URI** for an Azure AD application, it is important to know two things:
> - It should be unique across the tenant directory
> - If the application can become a multi-tenant application, a verified Azure AD domain must be used, in the form, `http://{tenant}.onmicrosoft.com/{appName}`

The result of this manual operation is the same as the automated operation performed by Visual Studio.

Inspecting messages

Using the preceding walkthrough does not give a real idea of what is going on between Azure AD and the web application. We have set up various assets but, to investigate what is passing through the wire, we can capture a sample web session.

To inspect what is going on, open Fiddler (refer to `http://www.telerik.com/fiddler`), then start the web application and perform the authentication as you do normally; as a result, this will appear:

2	302	HTTPS	localhost:44313	/
4	200	HTTPS	login.windows.net	/▮▮▮.onmicrosoft.com/FederationMetadata/2007...
6	302	HTTPS	login.windows.net	/▮▮▮.onmicrosoft.com/wsfed?wa=wsignin1.0&wt...
8	200	HTTPS	login.microsoftonlin...	/login.srf?wa=wsignin1.0&wtrealm=https%3a%2f%2flogin.windo...
9	200	HTTPS	login.microsoftonlin...	/GetUserRealm.srf?login=▮▮▮.onmicrosof...
10	200	HTTPS	login.microsoftonlin...	/ppsecure/post.srf?wa=wsignin1.0&wtrealm=https%3a%2f%2fl...
11	200	HTTPS	login.windows.net	/▮▮▮.onmicrosoft.com/wsfederation
16	302	HTTPS	localhost:44313	/
17	200	HTTPS	localhost:44313	/

Some sessions have been removed to highlight the interesting ones only

Here is what has happened:

- **Session 2**: The browser pointed to the web application
- **Session 4**: During the warm-up of the application, the Federation Metadata XML is downloaded, parsed, and partially saved, as explained before:

- **Session 6**: As the web application has been developed, a redirect to a login page happens immediately
- **Session 8**: The tenant-specific login page is shown to the user
- **Session 9**: While entering the username, Microsoft checks if it stands in the current tenant, otherwise it would change the realm

- **Session 10**: This is the POST step where the credentials have been validated against Microsoft's assets, setting some cookies on the response:

- **Session 11**: A security token is passed to the tenant-specific federation URL, which sets other cookies and passes the token to the application URL

- **Session 16**: The application URL is invoked with the security token, where a handler handles it and redirects it to the original URL.

In Session 11, we see the XML-based **Security Assertion Markup Language (SAML)** token, which is just one of the available formats we can use in this process.

Available claims and security groups

In the Federation Metadata Document, we can discover the available claims of the federation endpoint, so the claims that can be attached to the SAML token are returned to the web application:

 A complete reference for the Federation Metadata Document is at `https://msdn.microsoft.com/en-us/library/azure/dn195592.aspx`.

If we debug any authenticated page, we can inspect the identity, which has been injected into the current session, thereby discovering the actual available claims:

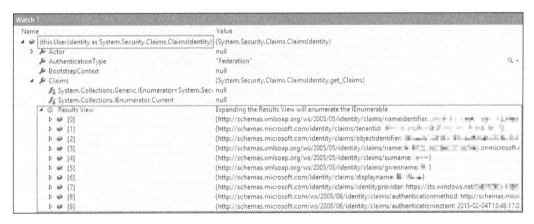

We can find interesting information, such as the tenant ID, object ID, usernames, first and last names, and so on. However, though the given user belongs to certain security groups, we do not find them in the available claims.

This is because, by default, the security groups' information is not passed to the relying party, except when we authorize it explicitly in the Azure AD application. This is not possible through the portal; however, we can directly edit the application manifest:

This is an excerpt of the manifest:

```
1   {
2       "allowActAsForAllClients": null,
3       "appId": "...",
4       "appMetadata": null,
5       "appRoles": [],
6       "availableToOtherTenants": false,
7       "displayName": "SingleTenantApplication",
8       "errorUrl": null,
9       "groupMembershipClaims": null,
10      "homepage": "https://localhost:44313/",
11      "identifierUris": [
12          "https://....onmicrosoft.com/SingleTenantApplication"
13      ],
```

We need to change "groupMembershipClaims" to "SecurityGroup" to pass the security groups as claims in the Token, as follows:

```
{http://schemas.microsoft.com/ws/2008/06/identity/claims/groups: ...}
{http://schemas.microsoft.com/ws/2008/06/identity/claims/groups: ...}
{http://schemas.microsoft.com/ws/2008/06/identity/claims/groups: ...}
```

In the figure, we see the claims of three groups, since the user is a member of three different security groups

Multi-tenant applications

Azure AD can be considered as a SaaS for IAM, before its relationship with Azure Services. A company that is offering its SaaS solution to clients can also use Azure AD as the Identity Provider, relying on the existing users of Office 365 (which relies on Azure AD for authentication) or Azure AD itself.

In the previous section, we see how to open an Azure AD application to use it within the boundaries of a single company; now, we see how to extend the pattern to multiple organizations with multi-tenant applications.

By using Visual Studio 2013, it is just a matter of the wizard being used, as done previously for a single-tenant application, by selecting **Cloud – Multiple Organizations**, as in this figure:

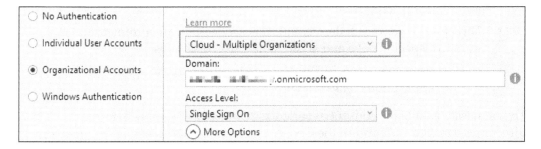

As a result of the project creation process, we have an almost identical project to the single-tenant application, with the difference being that the login URL will be in the `https://login.windows.net/common/wsfed` format.

The replacement of the tenant-specific part with the common part is due to the capability to accept users from outside the main directory where the application has been created.

The other difference is that, on the Azure AD side, the application is marked as multi-tenant, as in this figure:

Integration with other directories is now enabled; however, someone in the other directory should allow the third-party application to read its directory data, that is, the user's profiles.

Consent Framework

An application is unique (by its client ID) and it is always created in one directory. To enable a single sign-on for users outside the creation directory, a reference to the application must be created in the other directories as well. However, to do this, the explicit consent of an administrator of the directory must be acquired, so:

- Directory *A* creates the multi-tenant application; its users are automatically supported
- Directory *B* wants to federate with the application; an administrator goes to a specific page and accepts the trust conditions
    - ° After this, users in Directory *B* can authenticate against the application created in Directory *A*

To seamlessly enable the consent experience in a web application, external directories can sign up through the Consent URL, in the form, `https://account.activedirectory.windowsazure.com/Consent.aspx?ClientId=[ID]&RequestedPermissions=DirectoryReaders&ConsentReturnURL=`.

After the authentication, if a valid administrator is found, the following screen lets him or her decide whether to grant the application with the appropriate permissions:

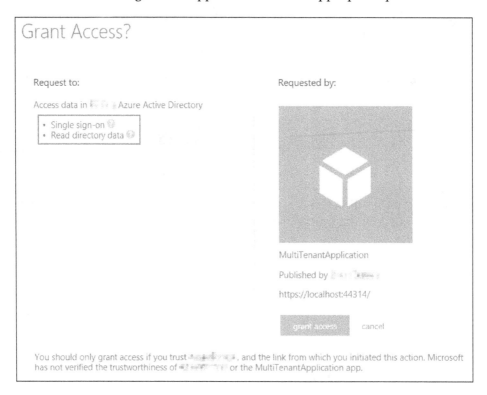

At the end of the process, this callback URL is usually called to let the application register the external tenant as trusted; you can refer to `https://[myapplicationUrl]/?Consent=Granted&TenantId=[ID]` for this.

From ASP.NET, we do not notice the differences between the two conditions (single-tenant versus multi-tenant), except for the value of the TenantID claim, whose value reflects the actual tenant, which is the authenticated current user.

Azure AD Graph API

The **Azure AD Graph API** provides programmatic access to Azure AD through the REST APIs; this is useful for many scenarios, such as:

- Performing **Create, Read, Update, and Delete (CRUD)** operations on the directory
- Getting/Setting additional properties of a user
- Implementing automation solutions

Generally, the Azure AD Graph API is very useful to integrate Azure AD with other scenarios in comparison to the ones officially explicated.

To access the Graph API via C#, we need:

- The **Active Directory Authentication Library (ADAL)** library for .NET
- The Azure AD Graph Client Library
- The proper application permission on the application
- Some settings, like the TenantID, the ClientID, and a valid ClientSecret

To enable an application to query the Azure AD Graph, we need to give the specific permission, **Read directory data**, as in this figure:

In addition to this, we need a valid secret key:

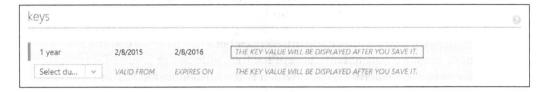

Given that we already know the basic settings (TenantID and ClientID), we can perform the setup of the Graph Client as follows:

```
var authority = "https://login.windows.net/[directory].onmicrosoft.
com";
Uri graphUri = new Uri("https://graph.windows.net");
Uri serviceRoot = new Uri(graphUri, tenantID);
ActiveDirectoryClient activeDirectoryClient = new
  ActiveDirectoryClient(serviceRoot, async () =>
  {
    AuthenticationContext ctx =
    new AuthenticationContext(authority);
    ClientCredential cred =
    new ClientCredential(clientID, clientSecret);
    AuthenticationResult auth =
    ctx.AcquireToken(graphUri.ToString(), cred);
    var token = auth.AccessToken;
    return token;
  });
```

The `async` lambda in the constructor of the `ActiveDirectoryClient` object is called once we require a protected resource from the directory, for example, the list of users, as follows:

```
var users = activeDirectoryClient.Users.ExecuteAsync()
  .Result.CurrentPage.ToArray();
```

To enable a read/write scenario, in the "permission to other applications" section of the Azure AD application configuration page, we can also specify "Read and write directory data".

Directory extensions

The Azure AD Directory Schema Extensions is a feature to add arbitrary properties to a directory's object to enable advanced scenarios or, generally, to enrich the directory information without requiring an external data store.

The current specifications of the feature are:

- Extensions can be registered to the following objects:
  - ○ User, group, TenantDetail, device, application, ServicePrincipal
- Extensions can be of the string (a maximum of 256 characters) or binary (a maximum 256 bytes) type
- A maximum of 100 registered extension properties can be written on a single directory's object across all applications

 This constraint means that, if an application writes 50 extension properties for a specific user, other applications can write only up to 50 more extension properties together.

Before writing the extension of an object, it must be registered on the application, as follows:

- Obtain a reference of the current application:

```
var currentApp = activeDirectoryClient
    .Applications.Where(p => p.AppId == clientID)
    .ExecuteSingleAsync().Result as Application;
```

- Add `ExtensionProperty`:

```
currentApp.ExtensionProperties.Add(new ExtensionProperty()
{
  Name = "ApplicationSpecificProp1",
  DataType = "String",
  TargetObjects = { "User" }
});
```

- Update the application:

```
currentApp.UpdateAsync().GetAwaiter().GetResult();
```

It is possible to obtain all the extension properties of a directory by calling this method:

```
var props = activeDirectoryClient
    .GetAvailableExtensionPropertiesAsync(false).Result;
```

Finally, since the `SetExtendedProperty` method is a method available on each `GraphObject`, every instance of it (that is, the user class) can attach properties, as follows:

1. Get the desired user:

```
var user = activeDirectoryClient.Users
    .Where(p => p
    .UserPrincipalName.StartsWith("UserToSearch"))
    .ExecuteSingleAsync().Result as User;
```

2. Write the extended property:

```
user.SetExtendedProperty("ApplicationSpecificProp1",
    "Test");
```

Azure AD has other powerful features that we do not cover here, such as differential query, an approach that returns all the changes made to entities during the time between two consecutive requests.

Azure AD Access Control Service

Azure AD Access Control Service (ACS) has been famous for a while for its capability to act as an identity bridge between applications and social identities. In the last few years, if developers wanted to integrate Facebook, Google, Yahoo, and a Microsoft account, (using a Live ID), respectively, they would have probably used ACS.

ACS is a middleware that centralizes authentication processes against multiple Identity Providers, as shown in the this figure:

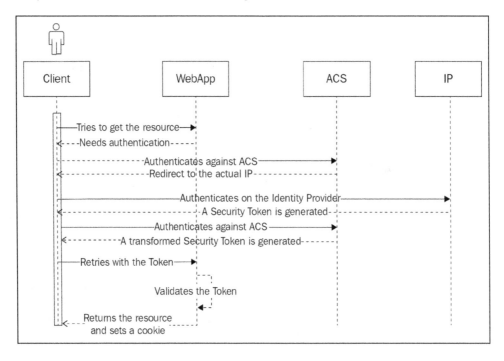

After ACS is properly configured to support multiple Identity Providers, the sample workflow is:

- A client requests a resource from the application
- The application tells the client to authenticate against ACS
- ACS tells the client to choose one of the supported Identity Providers
- The client then directly authenticates on the Identity Provider and gets a token
- The client shows the token to ACS
- ACS performs some "magic" and gives it the token to present to the application

Here, "magic" is a claims transformation process that is very valuable while dealing with multiple Identity Providers. Different Identity Providers use different claims. It is very important to make almost all the basic claims uniform before presenting them to the application, so as to avoid building custom software to manipulate them.

These are examples of the claims which are supported by different Identity Providers:

- **Facebook**: It includes the access token, e-mail address, expiration, name, and name identifier
- **Live ID**: It includes the name identifier
- **Yahoo**: It includes the e-mail address, name, and name identifier
- **Azure AD**: It includes the access token, display name, e-mail address, expiration, given name, groups, name identifier, and TenantID

In the following section, we implement the following scenario:

- A .NET application will use ACS to authenticate
- ACS will support Facebook, Microsoft account, and Azure AD as Identity Providers
- Users coming from Facebook and Microsoft account should be marked as **Guests** while Azure AD users must be put in the **User** role
- A specific Facebook user should be in the **Admin** role, including another specific user of Azure AD

Now, let's start with configuring ACS. To create a new ACS namespace, go to the current portal and, in the **ACCESS CONTROL NAMESPACES** tab of the **ACTIVE DIRECTORY** section, add a new namespace in an arbitrary location.

The management of ACS is performed outside the Azure Portal, by going to the URL `https://[namespaceName].accesscontrol.windows.net/v2/mgmt/web`. The `[namespaceName]` is the given name that should be used while creating the namespace.

Configuring Facebook as an Identity Provider

To configure Facebook as an Identity Provider, we need to create an application on Facebook, as follows:

1. Go to `https://developers.facebook.com/`.
2. Create a new website app with an arbitrary name and default settings.
3. Skip the optional steps and in the **Settings** page of the application, set:
   - App Domains: `[namespaceName].accesscontrol.windows.net`
   - Add the **Website** platform and write `https://[namespaceName].accesscontrol.windows.net` in the URL field
4. Copy the **App ID/API Key** and the **App Secret** to some other location.

In the ACS portal, locate the **Identity Providers** page and proceed as follows:

1. Click on **Add** and select the **Facebook application**.
2. Enter the **Application ID** and the **Application Secret** obtained before.
3. Leave `email` as the required permission.
4. Save the configuration.

Facebook is now configured as an Identity Provider for ACS. Refer to the Facebook documentation to learn how to use it in production, the regulations involved, and the terms of service.

Configuring Azure AD as an Identity Provider

Adding Azure AD as an Identity Provider for ACS is a very simple and straightforward operation. First, we need to create an Azure AD application. If you are coming from the previous sections, we can use the `SingleTenantApplication` defined before; otherwise, create a new application as specified in the *Single-tenant applications* section earlier in the chapter.

In the **CONFIGURE** tab of the `SingleTenantApplication`, locate the **Federation Metadata Document** endpoint:

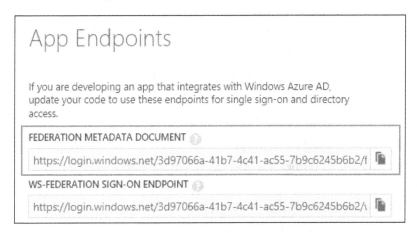

Before leaving the Azure AD application, change the **Sign-On URL**, the **App ID URI**, and the **Replay URL** to `https://[namespaceName].accesscontrol.windows.net/`.

In the ACS portal, locate the **Identity Providers** page and proceed as follows:

1. Click on **Add** and select **WS-Federation identity provider**.
2. In **Display name**, insert `Azure AD`.
3. Under **WS-Federation metadata**, paste the **URL** of the Azure AD application document.
4. In **Login link text**, enter `Azure AD` and save it.

Azure AD is now configured along with Facebook and Windows Live ID (the Microsoft account, which is configured by default).

Applying claims transformations

ACS supports the claims transformation for each application we set (also known as **relying party application**). A relying party application represents the actual web application we are going to create. To create a new relying party, proceed as follows:

1. Locate the **Relying Party Applications** section in the ACS management portal.
2. Add a new rely party application and fill in the fields, as follows:
   ° **Name**: Choose a name for the application

- ° **Realm**: Paste the base URL of the running application. During the Test/Dev period, it can be in the `https://localhost:port/` form
- ° **Return URL**: This is done as shown previously, but *remember to change both* with actual values while developing the application
- ° **Token format**: Leave **SAML 2.0**
- ° **Authentication Settings**: Leave all the **Identity Providers** checked (**Azure AD**, **Facebook**, and the **Windows Live ID**)
- ° **Rule groups**: Check **Create new rule group**

3. Save and locate the **Rule groups** section in the ACS management portal.
4. Select the group named **Default Rule Group for** X, where X is the ACS application name.
5. Generate the rules for the three supported Identity Providers.

A rule group is a group of transformation rules, which transform an incoming claim from the Identity Provider to an outgoing claim to present to the application. By generating the default rules for the Identity Providers, ACS creates a rule for each claim supported by the Identity Provider, as follows:

	Output Claim	Claim Issuer	Rule Description
☐	accesstoken	Azure AD	Passthrough "accesstoken" claim from Azure AD as "accesstoken"
☐	AccessToken	Facebook	Passthrough "AccessToken" claim from Facebook as "AccessToken"
☐	authenticationinstant	Azure AD	Passthrough "authenticationinstant" claim from Azure AD as "authenticationinstant"
☐	authenticationmethod	Azure AD	Passthrough "authenticationmethod" claim from Azure AD as "authenticationmethod"
☐	displayname	Azure AD	Passthrough "displayname" claim from Azure AD as "displayname"
☐	emailaddress	Facebook	Passthrough "emailaddress" claim from Facebook as "emailaddress"
☐	emailaddress	Azure AD	Passthrough "emailaddress" claim from Azure AD as "emailaddress"
☐	expiration	Facebook	Passthrough "expiration" claim from Facebook as "expiration"
☐	expiration	Azure AD	Passthrough "expiration" claim from Azure AD as "expiration"
☐	givenname	Azure AD	Passthrough "givenname" claim from Azure AD as "givenname"

1 of 3 ▶ ▶|

As we can see here, several rules are created. The majority are for the Azure AD provider, which supports many claims. In the target application, we need just two claim types:

- Unique identifier
- Roles

All three Identity Providers support the `nameidentifier` claim that can be used to uniquely identify the user in the application too. Now, we implement a claims transformation to inject a **Guest** role claim for users coming from Facebook or a Microsoft account:

- Remove all the rules, except the `nameidentifier` ones
- Add a new rule by adding the details as follows:
    - **Identity Provider**: Set this as **Facebook**
    - **Input claim type**: `http://schemas.xmlsoap.org/ws/2005/05/identity/claims/nameidentifier`
    - **Input claim value**: `Any`
    - **Output claim type**: `http://schemas.microsoft.com/ws/2008/06/identity/claims/role`
    - **Output claim value**: Set this as `Guest`
- Add a new identical rule for the Windows Live ID Identity Provider
- Add a new identical rule with the **Output claim value** set to `User` for the Azure AD Identity Provider

With these three rules, we generate a claim-based role, which will be injected in the ASP.NET pipeline through **Windows Identity Foundation (WIF)**, integrating the existing authorization workflow.

To set up the specification item, a specific Facebook user should be in the Admin role, as well as another specific user of Azure AD. Then, proceed as follows:

- Add a new rule for the Facebook Identity Provider by adding the details as follows:
    - **Input claim type**: `http://schemas.xmlsoap.org/ws/2005/05/identity/claims/emailaddress`
    - **Input claim value**: The Facebook e-mail address to make admin
    - **Output claim type**: `http://schemas.microsoft.com/ws/2008/06/identity/claims/role`

> ° **Output claim value**: Set this as `Admin`

- Add a new, similar rule for the Azure AD Identity Provider, specifying an actual AD user who should be made the administrator, using the input claim, `http://schemas.xmlsoap.org/ws/2005/05/identity/claims/name`

Integration with ASP.NET

The integration of ACS with ASP.NET is seamless, while using the Federation Metadata Document of ACS itself, as follows:

1. In the **Application Integration** page of the ACS management portal, copy the **WS-Federation Metadata** URL.

2. Create a new ASP.NET **MVC** web application.

3. While the wizard is running, click on **Change Authentication** and paste the URL in the box, as shown in this figure:

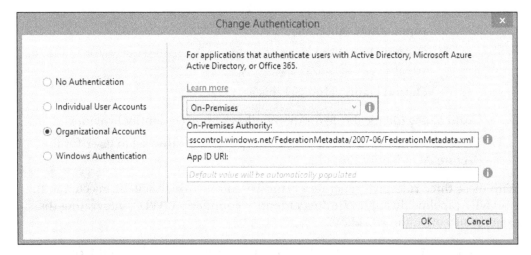

4. Put a breakpoint on the `Index()` action in the `HomeController` and run the solution.

5. Authenticate with the various providers and logins to verify the claims injection as we did in the previous section of the chapter.

6. Enjoy the integration by testing the validity of the existing authorization infrastructure, as shown in this code:

```
[Authorize(Roles="User")]
public ActionResult Index()
```

```
{
    return View();
}
```

ACS is a great feature that is used to simplify Identity Management, and Microsoft has stated that it would probably be integrated or extended into Azure AD in the near future.

Azure Key Vault

Azure **Key Vault** is a new promising service to store cryptographic keys and application secrets.

 At the time of writing this book, Azure Key Vault is still a preview service. Despite this, every service in Azure evolves at an incredible speed; this means that the procedures in this section are especially subject to major changes.

With the Key Vault, we come back to thinking about making thinks safer, thereby enabling certain scenarios, for example:

- We have a database connection string spread into several applications pointing to this database and we would like to:
    - Avoid writing it in certain configuration files
    - Prevent developers from having access to it
    - Avoid replicating/changing it in every deployment when the data source changes

- We have a Cryptographic Key that we use to sign several important documents and we would like to:
    - Avoid embedding it into the application
    - Sign documents without doing it on the application machine, so as to avoid the possibility of these documents being stolen

The first scenario is a general purpose scenario where some sort of secret has to be used in the application. However, if the secret is located outside the application in a central place, it is more maintainable than spreading it across the applications.

The second scenario is of primary importance for companies dealing with signing and encrypting processes. To sign/encrypt some payload, generally speaking, we need a payload, a key, and an encryption method. If we do this locally, the key should reside, before or later, on the memory of the machine that performs the operation. The Key Vault instead behaves like an encryption machine, taking the payload and the encryption method as an input, and produces the corresponding result as an output, though it never lets the key go outside its boundaries.

> In addition to this, using a specific pricing plan, we are guaranteed that the keys are kept in **Hardware Security Modules (HSMs)** and they never leave them.

Moreover, with its centrally managed architecture, the Key Vault enables logging around the access attempts to the secret and keys, improving the overall security as compared to a common implementation.

Creating a Key Vault

In this walkthrough, we see how to create a Key Vault and how to create a secret. For further information about Azure Key Vault, refer to `http://azure.microsoft.com/en-us/documentation/services/key-vault/`.

In order to proceed with the sample, we need:

- A subscription to Azure (the service pricing is available at `http://azure.microsoft.com/en-us/pricing/details/key-vault/`)
- Azure PowerShell version 0.8.13 or later version:
    - To check the current version of the Azure PowerShell module, use the `(Get-Module Azure).Version` command
- Azure Key Vault Scripts, available at `http://go.microsoft.com/fwlink/?linkid=521539&clcid=0x409`
- Azure Key Vault Client Libraries, available at `http://www.microsoft.com/en-us/download/details.aspx?id=45343`

Download and extract the Key Vault Scripts to a specific location, in order to use them later from PowerShell.

Creating the vault

A **vault** is a collection of secrets and keys; it is connected to a subscription and has a unique name worldwide in the form, `https://[name].vault.azure.net`.

Create a vault, as follows:

1. Connect your Azure accounts with the `Add-AzureAccount` cmdlet.

2. If you have multiple subscriptions, list them with the `Get-AzureSubscription` cmdlet.

3. Select the desired subscription with the `Select-AzureSubscription "[name]"` cmdlet.

4. Import the previously downloaded scripts with the `Import-Module "[path to the scripts]"` cmdlet.

> If a security error is raised, check the execution policy and, if needed, execute the `Set-ExecutionPolicy` cmdlet to change it to the appropriate level.

5. Switch the Azure Resource Manager mode with the `Switch-AzureMode AzureResourceManager` cmdlet.

6. Create the Key Vault with (`Demos` and `West Europe` are sample input) the `New-AzureKeyVault -VaultName "[name]" -ResourceGroupName "Demos" -Location "West Europe"` cmdlet.

As a result of this operation, a new Key Vault is created and a representing JSON is returned:

```
{
  "sku" : {
    "family" : "A",
    "name" : "standard"
  },
  "tenantId" : "[…]",
  "accessPolicies" : [
    {
      "tenantId" : "[…]",
      "objectId" : "[…]",
      "permissions" : {
        "secrets" : ["all"],
        "keys" : ["get", "create", "delete", "list", "update",
        "import", "backup", "restore"]
      }
```

```
        }
    ],
    "enabledForDeployment" : false,
    "vaultUri" : "https://[name].vault.azure.net/"
}
```

Note that the default `sku` of a Key Vault is *standard*, which does not offer HSM modules to store keys. To enable it, we need to create another Key Vault or delete/create the existing one, as follows:

```
New-AzureKeyVault -VaultName "[name]" -ResourceGroupName "Demos" -
    Location "West Europe" -Sku premium
```

Now, we will see how to add a key and a secret to the Key Vault.

Adding a key or secret

A Key Vault can store keys in order to provide further operations around it. To store the existing key of an existing PFX file, proceed as follows:

1. Locate the PFX file and its protection password.

2. Wrap the password in a `SecureString`, as follows:

   ```
   $passwd=ConvertTo-SecureString -String "packt" -AsPlainText -
       Force
   ```

3. Add the key to the HSM module, as follows:

   ```
   $key=Add-AzureKeyVaultKey -VaultName "[vaultName]" -Name
       "[keyName]" -KeyFilePath "[path]\file.pfx" -KeyFilePassword
       $passwd -Destination HSM
   ```

4. Verify the unique URI of the key just created with:

   ```
   $key.Id
   ```

To create a secret, proceed as follows:

1. Wrap the secret in a SecureString, as follows:

   ```
   $secretString=ConvertTo-SecureString -String "password" -
       AsPlainText -Force
   ```

2. Add the secret to the Key Vault, as follows:

   ```
   $secret=Set-AzureKeyVaultSecret -VaultName "[vaultName]" -Name
       "[secretName]" -SecretValue $secretString
   ```

3. Verify the unique URI of the key just created with:

`$secret.Id`

Adding the same key or secret multiple times results in a new version. The unique URI of a key or secret is in this form:

```
https://[vaultName].vault.azure.net/keys/[keyName]/[versionGuid]
```

The `versionGuid` changes each time the key or secret is changed. To reference the current version of a key or secret, only its name is required:

```
https://[vaultName].vault.azure.net/secrets/[secretName]
```

To reference a specific version of a key or secret, the full URI is required.

Using the .NET client library

There is an official library to operate against Key Vault from .NET, using Azure AD authentication to get secrets or to use the keys. Before using it, it is necessary to set appropriate permissions on the Key Vault for external access, using the `Set-AzureKeyVaultAccessPolicy` command. The command can authorize:

- A specific user of the tenant directory
- An application of the Azure AD tenant

To grant `sign` privileges to a specific user, use the following command:

```
Set-AzureKeyVaultAccessPolicy -VaultName [vaultName] -
  UserPrincipalName [userOfTheDirectory] -PermissionsToKeys sign
```

To grant `all` privileges to a specific application by its Client ID, use the following command:

```
Set-AzureKeyVaultAccessPolicy -VaultName [vaultName] -
  ServicePrincipalName [clientID] -PermissionsToSecrets all
```

 Note that the current logged PowerShell user must be able to enumerate directory objects, in order to complete the operation below. If the message **No object ID for the input principal was found** is shown, consider investigating the actual permission of the user against the directory (if it is an external account, for instance, be sure the **LIMIT GUEST ACCESS** is set to **YES**).

After that, we can open Visual Studio and proceed as follows:

- Create a new console application
- Add references to the client libraries projects in:
    - ○ `Microsoft.KeyVault.Client`
    - ○ `Microsoft.KeyVault.WebKey`
- Write this code to authenticate on Azure AD:

```
var vaultName = "https://[vaultName].vault.azure.net";
KeyVaultClient client = new KeyVaultClient(
  new KeyVaultClient.AuthenticationCallback
((authority, resource, scope) =>
  {
    var clientID = "[clientID]";
    var clientSecret = "[clientSecret]";
    var clientCredential =
    new ClientCredential(clientID, clientSecret);
    var ctx = new AuthenticationContext(authority, null);
    var result = ctx.AcquireToken(resource,
    clientCredential);
    return result.AccessToken;
  }),setRequestUriCallback:(uri,httpClient)=>uri);
```

- Add this line to enumerate secrets:

```
IEnumerable<SecretItem> secret =
  client.GetSecretsAsync(vaultName).Result;
```

- Add this code to get individual secret values:

```
var firstValue =
  client.GetSecretAsync(secret.First().Id).Result.Value;
```

Many features are already available in the client library, but since they can change a lot until general assembly, it is better to refer to the official Key Vault page, `http://azure.microsoft.com/services/key-vault`.

Summary

In this chapter, we talked about Azure AD as a great resource while developing applications that need an IAM solution and we discovered the interesting role of ACS as a collector of Identity Providers.

We used Key Vault to create a secure place to store keys and secrets and we investigated some practices to use it from the applications.

Index

Symbol

.NET client library
using 123, 124

A

Access Control Lists (ACLs) 25
Access Control Service (ACS)
about 71, 112
Azure AD, configuring as Identity
    Provider 114, 115
claims transformations, applying 115-117
Facebook, configuring as Identity
    Provider 114
implementation 113
integrating, with ASP.NET 118, 119
workflow 113
Account keys 57, 58
**Active Directory Authentication
    Library (ADAL) 109**
advanced authentication
about 33
Management Certificate 36
Multi-Factor Authentication 34
affinity cookie 48
Application Program Interface (API) 47
Application Request Routing (ARR) 48
app passwords 28
ASP.NET
ACS, integrating 118, 119
Authentication apps
reference link 34

authenticator app 29
Azure Active Directory (Azure AD)
about 23, 96
ACS 112
application, integrating 99
claims-based authentication 96-99
configuring, as Identity Provider 114, 115
Graph API 109, 110
groups, creating 25
multi-tenant applications 99, 106, 107
single-tenant applications 99-102
user access, configuring 25
users, creating 25
Azure AD Graph API
about 109, 110
directory extensions 110, 111
Azure AD, options
Authentication apps 34
Automated phone calls 34
Automated SMS messages 34
Azure Backup
about 90
backup vault, configuring 91
schedule, backing up 92, 93
server, registering 92
URL, for restoration process 93
Azure Linux Agent
reference link 77

B

backups, Websites 55, 56
breach 2
Bring Your Own Device (BYOD) 11

C

cache
  about 66
  Managed Cache 66
  Redis Cache 69
Chief Information Security Officer (CISO) 4
CIA triangle
  about 2, 3
  availability 2
  confidentiality 2
  integrity 2
claims-based authentication, Azure AD
  about 96-99
  claim 96
  identity 96
Classless Inter-Domain Routing (CIDR) 79
Cloud-only VNet 86
Cloud Services
  about 40
  Microsoft Antimalware 45, 46
  network communication 46, 47
  Remote Desktop 42, 43
  remote endpoints 40-42
  startup tasks 44
co-administrator
  adding, to subscription 26
code, hosting
  about 39
  Cloud Services 40
  Websites 47-49
code of conduct 10
compliance
  implementing 19
connection modes, Websites 52
connection strings, Websites 52-55
Consent Framework 108, 109
Create, Read, Update, and Delete (CRUD) operations 109
credentials, Websites
  about 49
  example 51
  site-level credentials 50
  user-level credentials 50
cross-premises VNet 86
Custom Application 96

custom Azure Active Directory
  creating 23, 24
Customer Relationship Management (CRM) 4

D

datacenter 17
data, hosting
  about 57
  SQL Database 61, 62
  Storage 57
Denial of Service (DoS) 11
directory extensions, Azure AD Graph API
  about 110
  obtaining 111
  specifications 110
Distributed Denial of Service (DDoS) 19
due care 4
due diligence 4

E

encryption 12
Entity Framework (EF) 54
ExpressRoute 89
Extended Key Usage (EKU) 91
extension 42
extensions, Websites
  about 56
  native (or preinstalled) 56
  third-party (private or from a gallery) 56
  URL 56
external security, Virtual Machines
  about 75
  ACLs 78, 79
  endpoints 78, 79
  extensions 82, 83
  isolation 80, 81
  networking 80, 81
  Windows, versus Linux 75-77

F

Facebook
  configuring, as Identity Provider 114
Federation Metadata Document
  reference link 105

T

Transport Layer Security (TLS) 52
two-step verification
    setting up 28, 29

U

user-level credentials 50

V

vault
    about 121
    creating 121, 122
Virtual Hard Disk (VHD) 76
Virtual Machines
    about 16, 75
    external security 74-83
    internal security 74, 83-85
Virtual Networks (VNets)
    about 74, 86
    hybrid networks 89
    Network Security Groups (NSG) 87-89
Virtual Private Network (VPN) 4
VM Depot
    about 77
    reference link 77

W

Web Deploy
    reference link 43
    using 43
web role 40
Websites
    about 47-49
    backups 55, 56
    connection modes 52
    connection strings 52-55
    credentials 49, 50
    extensions 56
    Project Kudu 49
    settings 52-55
Windows Identity Foundation (WIF) 117
worker role 40

X

XML Document Transformation (XDT) 56

About Packt Publishing

Packt, pronounced 'packed', published its first book, *Mastering phpMyAdmin for Effective MySQL Management*, in April 2004, and subsequently continued to specialize in publishing highly focused books on specific technologies and solutions.

Our books and publications share the experiences of your fellow IT professionals in adapting and customizing today's systems, applications, and frameworks. Our solution-based books give you the knowledge and power to customize the software and technologies you're using to get the job done. Packt books are more specific and less general than the IT books you have seen in the past. Our unique business model allows us to bring you more focused information, giving you more of what you need to know, and less of what you don't.

Packt is a modern yet unique publishing company that focuses on producing quality, cutting-edge books for communities of developers, administrators, and newbies alike. For more information, please visit our website at www.packtpub.com.

About Packt Enterprise

In 2010, Packt launched two new brands, Packt Enterprise and Packt Open Source, in order to continue its focus on specialization. This book is part of the Packt Enterprise brand, home to books published on enterprise software – software created by major vendors, including (but not limited to) IBM, Microsoft, and Oracle, often for use in other corporations. Its titles will offer information relevant to a range of users of this software, including administrators, developers, architects, and end users.

Writing for Packt

We welcome all inquiries from people who are interested in authoring. Book proposals should be sent to author@packtpub.com. If your book idea is still at an early stage and you would like to discuss it first before writing a formal book proposal, then please contact us; one of our commissioning editors will get in touch with you.

We're not just looking for published authors; if you have strong technical skills but no writing experience, our experienced editors can help you develop a writing career, or simply get some additional reward for your expertise.

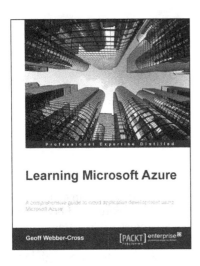

Learning Microsoft Azure

ISBN: 978-1-78217-337-3   Paperback: 430 pages

A comprehensive guide to Cloud application development using Microsoft Azure

1. Build, deploy, and host scalable applications in the Cloud using Windows Azure.

2. Enhance your mobile applications to receive notifications via the notifications Hub.

3. Features a full enterprise Azure case study with detailed examples and explanations.

Microsoft Azure Development Cookbook

Second Edition

ISBN: 978-1-78217-032-7   Paperback: 422 pages

Over 70 advanced recipes for developing scalable services with the Microsoft Azure platform

1. Understand, create, and use the hosting services of Azure for processing and storage.

2. Explore different approaches to implement scalable systems by using Azure services.

3. Pick the appropriate automation strategy and minimize management efforts.

Please check **www.PacktPub.com** for information on our titles

Mastering System Center Configuration Manager

Mastering System Center Configuration Manager

ISBN: 978-1-78217-545-2   Paperback: 278 pages

Master how to configure, back up, and secure access to System Center Configuration Manager with this practical guide

1. Employ fast and scalable on-demand application deployment.

2. Discover the best practices to utilize faster and more efficient anti-malware scanning of clients.

3. Packed with easy and practical examples to improve your asset management quickly and effectively.

Visual Studio 2013 and .NET 4.5 Expert Cookbook

ISBN: 978-1-84968-972-4   Paperback: 308 pages

Over 30 recipes to successfully mix the powerful capabilities of Visual Studio 2013 with .NET 4.5

1. Provides step-by-step instructions, helping you to learn the various components and technologies of .NET development with Visual Studio 2013.

2. Filled with examples that clearly illustrate how to integrate with the technologies and frameworks of your choice.

3. Helps you keep pace with the fast growing IT industry and gain expertise on upcoming technologies, common forms of debugging and software testing.

Please check **www.PacktPub.com** for information on our titles

www.ingramcontent.com/pod-product-compliance
Lightning Source LLC
Chambersburg PA
CBHW082120070326
40690CB00049B/4004